Marshal Ney's
Military Studies

MARSHAL NEY

Marshal Ney's Military Studies

Battlefield Tactics and Army Organisation During the Napoleonic Age

ILLUSTRATED

Marshal Ney

Translated by
G. H. Caunter

LEONAUR

Marshal Ney's Military Studies
Battlefield Tactics and Army Organisation During the Napoleonic Age
by Marshal Ney
Translated by G. H. Caunter

ILLUSTRATED

First published under the title
Military Studies

Leonaur is an imprint of Oakpast Ltd

Copyright in this form © 2021 Oakpast Ltd

ISBN: 978-1-78282-924-9 (hardcover)
ISBN: 978-1-78282-925-6 (softcover)

http://www.leonaur.com

Contents

To

The Officers of the British Army,
Regulars, Militia, and Yeomanry,
On the Old Roman Maxim That,
"*Fas est etiam ab hoste doceri*"
This Translation of
Marshal Ney's Military Studies
Is Respectfully Inscribed

MICHEL NEY, 1792,
AS A YOUNG OFFICER OF THE 4TH HUSSARS

Introduction
By A. James.
Late Major 67th Regiment.

In giving a translation of Marshal Ney's *Military Studies*—an officer not only *le plus brave des braves*, but justly celebrated for his talents, as well as for the accuracy of his evolutions, and the precision and simplicity of his formations,—it is not intended to impugn the principles of British tactics, nor to derogate from the lofty pretensions and unquestioned merit of the great founder of the British system—a system which has stood the test of practical experience in peace and in war—a system scientifically erected on sound and true principles, and which will long remain a splendid testimony of the zeal, genius, and prodigious industry of its illustrious architect.

But admirable as that system is, it would be too much to assume that it is not susceptible of improvement. Bigots may brawl, "Great is Diana of the Ephesians," but Englishmen will not forget that it was by acting on the liberal maxim, *fas est etiam ab hoste doceri* , that Rome became mistress of the world! Highly and deservedly as we appreciate our own system, military men will probably discover in the few but masterly movements of the great tactician whose Studies are here presented to them, something that may enlarge their views, and even benefit the service.

Marshal Ney, an eminent general, seriously devoted to his profession, does not seem to have contemplated the gorgeous display of a review, the pomp of a field-day, nor even a dress parade, as constituting the most brilliant points of a soldier's life, or the most important object, the *ne plus ultra* of military science and professional attainments! His Grace the Archbishop of Canterbury in his charge, says—and he says it to their praise:

> Our forefathers understood the nature and value of a spiritual worship; they abolished useless foundations, and expelled from their church the gaudy decorations and ceremonial pageantry which diverted the attention of the people from the proper objects.

This high and elegant encomium may, *mutatis mutandis*, with great propriety be applied to the lamented officer whose unassuming labours are now before the public. His manoeuvres are grounded on the most unerring and simple principles. The presence of an enemy is always supposed—they have all a direct relation and reference to the field, and are such as may be required and practised on the most critical occasions. They combine in a high degree the great *desiderata* of celerity, facility, justness, and security, which gives them a legitimate claim to the favourable consideration of the soldier who is honestly ambitious to shine in his profession.

It was at first intended to have illustrated every one of the movements by corresponding elucidatory diagrams;—for, as the intelligent Salden well observes:

> The ideas are formed much quicker upon a plan, than from the best relation without a drawing; because the eye may follow the manoeuvres, as if one was present at them.

But it was found that such a plan would materially tend to swell the expense of the work; indeed, it would have defeated the main object of the publisher, which was to offer to the British Army, regulars and militia, a neat and cheap edition of the marshal's *Military Studies*, in an English dress. Diagrams of a few of the principal movements only have therefore been given.

In the technical terms and expressions, purely military, the translator has been solicitous to preserve, as far as possible, the peculiar phraseology and spirit of his original. Thus, the words, *guides, conversion*, &c. &c. have frequently; been retained, and will of course be readily understood.

And although the marshal's movements are, in general, arranged for four regiments of two battalions, on two lines, each battalion consisting of four divisions, or eight *pelotons*—yet the principles are the same; and, with a few obvious alterations, the explanations strictly apply to any evolution upon a smaller or a larger scale: for the mode of execution, being based on fixed principles, remains unchangeable. It is wished to draw the particular attention of intelligent military readers to the valuable remarks of the marshal on squares, and on his varied methods of formation. His remarks on oblique formations, on movements in echelons of battalions, on refusing a flank, and operations of second lines, are also masterly, and worthy of notice.

From a careful examination of the *Studies* before us, it will at once be evident that *simplicity* and *security* were the great objects which that celebrated officer had constantly in view. In his manoeuvres we find nothing complex, nothing that can induce uncertainty, perplexity, or confusion, nothing *recherché*, nothing pedantically finical; utility is never sacrificed to show—no loose desultory movements, accidental modes, and caprice—no frippery heterogeneous formations—no fancy evolutions—which, wherever and to whatever extent they are allowed to prevail, must need subvert that unity and uniformity of system, without which valour alone will not ensure victory, and even the manly daring of an army may lead them to destruction.

In eulogising *Les Etudes Militaires* of Marshal Ney, we are not blind to the excellence and value of British tactics. For though under the auspices of a prince, by whose honourable zeal and unwearied exertions the armies of England were raised to that unprecedented state of efficiency and discipline which, leaving nothing to chance, chained victory to their banners;—yet, let it not be forgotten, that it was the system of Dundas which, inspiring the soldier with confidence, and arraying with unconquerable force the native energy and courage of the British character, enabled Britain, in the late long and tremendous struggle, to come off "more than conqueror," and to cover herself with glory.

And though "a lapse of thirty-three years had rendered a revision of that venerable system necessary," it is pleasing to remark, that the introduction affixed to the new system of field exercise, strenuously upholds, and reverentially consecrates, the fundamental principles of Sir David Dundas's stupendous fabric. This is liberal, and it is just. It reflects honour on that talented and universally esteemed officer, now no more, by whom the present regulations were with much labour prepared. But military men will readily concede, that this new system is very susceptible of improvement.

Dundas has spots indeed, but consider his brilliancy! And though it is certain that the last eventful war did suggest some amendments, yet it has become matter of question with many military men of great eminence, whether those amendments might not have been infused into the system without so much change. The increased celerity in the mode of executing the movements, which has with much tact been introduced, is confessedly a very material improvement, though even that should be discretely regulated.

We are not aware, however, that the mighty structure of that distinguished veteran has in many other respects been really advanced; and it is sincerely to be hoped, that the zeal and exertions of succeeding generations will be applied and limited to the great object of *maintaining the magnificent structure of Dundas in its original splendour and beauty.* Where are the modern architects, however celebrated and scientific, who could with any prospect of success, and without temerity, undertake to remodel or amend that venerable pile, "those clustering columns, those vaulted roofs, those lofty towers," which arrest the admiration of the stranger, and are to this day the wonder of the age, and the glory of the metro-political see?

Bearing in mind what the armies of Britain have achieved, amid circumstances of extreme difficulty and peril, under that system, which in the hands of our high-minded soldiers has proved at once the buckler and the spear; it is, in truth, no wonder that military men should be ardently wedded to it, and that doubts and apprehensions should have been entertained as to the expediency of the improvements stated to have been suggested by practical experience.

When you propose to cut away the rotten parts, can you

tell us what are perfectly sound? Are there any certain limits, in fact or theory, to inform you at what point you must stop?

The mere application of *increased celerity* to the movements of the great military machine, which was required, might have been effected by substituting *quick* for *ordinary*, and in a few cases *double quick* for *quick time*—but beyond that we should have trembled to proceed.

Where, for instance, is the wisdom—where the advantage of those endless and cumbrous formations of *threes* and *fours*, which give an air of bustle and confusion, especially when applied "to the internal movements and formations of the divisions of a battalion, and to the flank movements of battalions in columns of manoeuvre?" Are they even ornamental? Are they military? *Threes right—threes left—threes inwards—threes outwards*; and *rear form four deep—left form four deep—right form four deep*—with all the ungainly and unprofitable mechanism therewith unavoidably connected, if not formally abrogated by authority, should be allowed to fall into disuse.

Such formations require the men to be particularly *told off, the files numbered;* and though on parade, where files are in no danger of being put *hors de combat*, such formations might be endured; yet, *as nothing should be practised in the barrack square that has not a reference to the field, even there they might with good taste be dispensed with.*

When we are told that *this formation* and *march* "afford the advantage of moving the divisions of a battalion in compact order towards their several points of formation, upon a space within the extent of their front, and that the double time can be conveniently applied, whereas *file marching* is liable to extension;" we should be content to admit the plausibility of the argument, if soldiers, when once located in companies, numbered and told off, remained each *in suo loco*, like the son of Peleus, invulnerable. With the new regulations we say, that formations by *threes*, &c. are liable to repeated derangement, which casualties in action may cause in *the telling off*, and which in our opinion all the attention of all the supernumerary officers and sergeants in the rear to correct the breaks, and renew as often as may be this *general telling off*, will certainly fail to remedy.

Nor can we concede that this probable, nay unavoidable inconvenience, is counterbalanced by the advantages above enumerated. We are for utterly discontinuing all these ponderous *threes* and *fours*:—*file marchings* with its magnified inherent vicious propension, has served our turn, and would again be found fully sufficient to ensure precision, provided the men were properly practised and steadied in it.

In shadowing out these objections, we are aware they are as mere spots on the glorious disk of the sun—mere blemishes, which, considering the intrinsic beauty and excellence of the British system, sink into insignificance. Who, indeed, can sufficiently eulogise a system which, during an anxious and protracted period of eventful operations, involving the very fate of our country, has never failed or deceived us; never failed to shed lustre on our arms, and like *the pillar of a cloud* and *the pillar of fire*, never ceased to lead Britons to glory and to victory! We venture to indicate these blemishes (if blemishes they are) solely for the purpose of more distinctly marking the grounds on which we so highly appreciate the system of Dundas.

Like the *Studies* of Marshal Ney, the system of the British general is founded on indestructible principles; it embraces everything that is valuable—it is just in all its movements, determined, and accurate in its details; and though its *procession* was found to be too slow to keep pace with the increased velocity of the accelerated systems of neighbouring states, that, we submit, might have been rectified without altering a single section, or reconstructing a single manoeuvre.

And though every regiment should be well practised in the whole range of necessary evolutions, yet it may perhaps occur to the reflecting officer that, for purposes of reviews or inspections, certain of the most useful and important movements, selected and regulated by authority, as best calculated to try the steadiness and discipline of the men and the intelligence of the officers, might with manifest advantage have been retained.

The *Studies* of the French marshal present in general mere

indications of manoeuvres, yet even in these sketches we see the hand of a master. They are mere outlines, mere silhouettes in fact, but, like the cartoons of Raphael, they constitute a monument which bids fair to be *aere perennius!* Soldiers of genius, finished tacticians, like poets and painters, are seldom seen; and if in an age a Dundas appear in Britain, or a Prince de la Moskowa on the Continent, their labours become the property of the world, and, like the sacred fire of the temple, should be religiously preserved! The study and comprehension of the marshal's manoeuvres suppose a previous knowledge of at least the rudiments and leading principles of the profession.

But it is a preposterous conceit, fatal to military attainment, that officers have nothing to do with any tactics but their own!—that the study of evolutions should be exclusively confined to officers of rank! The fundamentals of the profession, in all its branches, become not only a proper but an indispensable study for every officer, high or low, who aspires to a due knowledge of his

Though Marshal Ney's *Studies* are too much an *epitome* to convey sufficient detailed instruction on the various objects he discusses, yet, even so, they will be perused with interest, and certainly not without advantage. The translator will be gratified if his anxious desire to render this publication worthy of public patronage, has not been defeated by want of ability to catch the spirit of the original, without which it can have no merit in the eyes of judges so competent.

These *Military Studies* were evidently not constructed, nor are they now published, under the ostentatious denomination of a complete system. At the time they were arranged, the French tactics appear to have been singularly defective, "mere straw and stubble."—"*Les manoeuvres préscrites par l'ordonnance sur l'instruction de 1791*," were by no means of a high order; and though the *enthusiastic spirit*, which passed then under the name of "*l'amour sacré de la patrie*," and which, like a meteor, flashed through France under the stirring and exciting scenes of that revolutionary convulsion which shattered the throne, threw down the altars, and deluged the country with the blood of her citizens, was for a while accounted to them for discipline, and for a time stood them in the stead of subordination and military training; yet Marshal Ney was soon convinced that all this would rapidly evaporate, *and that without discipline there is no safety for an army.*

He therefore applied himself early and strenuously to the rectification of the military principles, and to the amendment of the then existing regulations. His *Studies, "dont l'expérience lui préscrit de préferer l'usage,"* were plainly intended to give instruction, and with instruction confidence, to the soldier. For, as he pertinently observes:

> *La confiance de la troupe dans la supériorité de sa tactique les rendra toujours plus ou moins satisfaisans, et maintiendra, avec cette reputation, l'honneur des régimens, et la gloire des armes de l'empire."*

The confidence of the troop in the superiority of its tactics will always make them more or less satisfactory, and will maintain, with this reputation, the honour of the regiments, and the glory of the arms of the empire.

These reflections of a brave, an intelligent, a patriotic, and, in his death, unfortunate officer—this last legacy of the renowned Duc d'Elchingen, will not fail to prove valuable. His maxims are sound, his arrangements excellent, his views comprehensive, though not always clearly expressed. Many of his formations have been adopted, and actually constitute the most valuable portion of the French regulations; and the publishers will be gratified if the plan they have adopted of offering to the army this portion of Ney's *Memoirs* in a separate volume shall prove deserving of their patronage.

It will of course be recollected that these *Studies* were written for the use of Marshal Ney's own officers, and not with a view to publication. When the marshal commanded the camp at Montreuil-sur-Mer, in 1804, having practically experienced the insufficiency of the regulations then in force, and seeing the necessity of instructing the officers under his command, he had a spacious room constructed in the rear of each regiment, which he designated the officers' council-room. Here the officers of the respective corps, from the colonel to the youngest subaltern, were obliged to meet and study their profession together; the marshal's idea being that solitary study often tends to error, which by public and general study and discussion may in most cases be obviated. Each officer was called upon to give an explanation of every manoeuvre in which he had taken a share in battle, discuss its utility, its advantages, &c.

Ney would then briefly offer his own ideas, and argue each point familiarly with his comrades. These rooms were, in fact, regimental schools for tactics. The marshal regularly attended the council-room of every regiment in rotation, and generally gave out subjects for study. It was in this view, and for this object, that he wrote a great many papers on tactics, but, at the moment, without any other motive than the laudable desire of instructing his officers, and making them conversant with his own evolutions; and he had the satisfaction to see that his labour was not in vain—for Ney's officers were confessedly the best instructed, the most ready, and intelligent in the army.

The *Military Studies* here given are only a portion of the articles he thus prepared for his officers. Ney commanded the "left division" of the army, as it was then termed. But with great propriety his writings may be denominated *General Instructions for the Army*.

Whilst the translator has endeavoured to feel his way through those difficulties, and illustrate those almost inextricably perplexing laconisms and abstrusity of expression, which not unfrequently obscure the pages of his author, he has been anxious to catch a portion of that redeeming spirit which marks almost every period of the original. The valuable and ofttimes brilliant evolutions which, in view to practical application, Marshal Ney contemplated, seem to have been familiar to his mind, and lucidly shadowed out in his imagination, though he did not always sufficiently consider, even in his council-rooms, that what to him appeared distinct and evident, might with others require considerable elucidation and detail.

Actively employed in the service of his country, he had little leisure for the above studies, and the marvel is, not that he wrote so little, but that he wrote at all; not that his manoeuvres are limited, his studies without amplitude—but that, amid the toils, and bustle, and anxieties of war and of command, he could find a moment for the pen. From Marshal Ney, under such circumstances, the world could hardly have expected an elaborate system of tactics.

Ney, like Dundas, has too often delivered himself either in objectionably compendious, or in vague and ambiguous terms; he wanted leisure to apply his ideas to the methodical development of his projected operations. Indeed, it may be lamented, that to their many and splendid talents they have not generally united that happy *perspicuity* so essential in works of science, and which the important nature of their studies specially demanded. Yet, with all his defects, Dundas has nobly embraced the totality of his profession, established British tactics, and deserved well of the state; and though the *Military Studies* of Ney are comparatively a mere epitome, he too is admirable; his works are those of a master,—they cannot be mistaken; they evidently bear the impress of military genius; and if the value of his literary labours may be estimated by his reputation as a soldier, he too will be read with pleasure and advantage.

Differing in magnitude, their systems are erected on the same unalterable principles. Dundas, under favourable auspices, framed, from its first elements to its most complex formations, a complete and stupendous system for the armies of Britain. Ney, in the hurry of the moment, promulgates a few leading manoeuvres, a few military studies for the immediate use of his own officers.

Dundas wrote and studied in his closet—Ney in the tented field. Dundas is laborious, plodding, minute, slow, and precise— sometimes prolix, sometimes, like Homer, he even nods on the march; Ney conceives with the rapidity of lightning, but flags in the detail, and seldom imparts his conceptions with clearness—his sword was the sword of Caesar, but his pen is the pen of Dundas: regardless of *minutiae* he rushes on to the *finale*; and rarely shines, even in the council-room, in the work of explanation. And thus it happens, as pertinently observed by an eminent writer, that those who labour to be brief sometimes become obscure—"*brevis esse laboro , obscurus fro.*"

If then, amid all these disadvantages, without presuming to flatter himself that he has succeeded in freeing his version from all perplexity and entanglement, the translator has preserved the form and structure of his own vernacular language without falling into *English French*;—if, upon the whole, he has been faithful to his original, and not altogether misapprehended his military terms, he may perhaps be permitted to appeal to a British public, and to the British Army in particular, not for applause, for that is the legitimate reward of originality and of genius, but for as much of their approbation as in their wonted liberality they may judge a faithful translator fairly entitled to.

Of Marshal Ney, as a tactician, it is impossible to speak in language too eulogical. With the merits or demerits of his conduct in regard to Louis the XVIIIth and Napoleon,—and the policy or impolicy of his tragical end,—we have here nothing to do; but so long as he is universally allowed by friends and foes to have displayed wonderful intelligence of his subject, superior proofs of tactical power, and given useful and excellent evolutions, he may well be forgiven his want of literary polish and Ciceronian elegance.

Under the auspices of Lord Hill, an officer from his rank and talents pre-eminently qualified correctly to decide on the relative merits of military tactics, it is not unreasonable to indulge the expectation that the British system, grounded as it is on sound and inexpugnable principles, will yet be subjected to such scrutinising revision as may tend to a *restoration* of Dundas in all his original simplicity. That system was peculiarly suited to the national character—under that system the native courage, the patriotic ardour of Britons was ever most powerfully elicited. Armed and inspired by the spirit of that system, his Majesty's armies became literally invincible. Arrayed in the high-wrought panoply of that system, Britons redeemed the sinking, the almost desperate, fortunes of Europe—finally crushed the modern Caesar of his age, and all his lofty projects of universal dominion, and gave peace to the world.

If it is natural "to speak well of the bridge that safely bears us over," let it not be accounted irrational to vindicate the system which, under unexampled perils, secured our independence, exalted the reputation of our armies, and immortalised our fame.

To Lord Hill then, who bore so prominent a part in these splendid achievements, so distinguished apart in the battles of his country, and who must have had many and signal occasions of *witnessing the peculiar excellence and buoyancy of the British system*, I am encouraged to appeal, whether the encomiums I have ventured to pass on that system are or are not borne out by facts. Nor will the appeal be made in vain.

I now close this humble, though honestly intended Introduction to the *Military Studies* of an officer who, whatever may have been his errors and his misfortunes, will be read with advantage.

Accelerate, if you will, the movements of the system; but not, in the language of *reform,—Let us have Dundas, all Dundas, and nothing but Dundas!* I will not exclaim with the enthusiast, "*errare malo cum Platone, quam cum istis rectè sentire*," for with Dundas as a guide, I verily believe it will be impossible to go wrong.

Military Studies

INSTRUCTIONS FOR THE TROOPS COMPOSING THE LEFT CORPS.
(General Schneider, member of the Military Board in France, has been so good as to read Marshal Ney's manuscript, and to indicate the points of similarity between these studies and the changes adopted in the new infantry regulations. The notes by this general are distinguished by an S.)

The generals of division, in superintending the drilling of the several regiments under their command, will be pleased to apply, to the principal evolutions in line hereinafter described, the observations which I have made upon each, whether with a view to obtain all possible celerity and precision in the movements required in the execution of such evolutions, or to simplify some of them, or to compare the manoeuvres prescribed in the drill regulations of 1791 with those more commonly in use in the field, and which experience teaches us to prefer.

There is no general officer of the present day who does not admit the advantage of acting in the field with troops skilled in the execution of great manoeuvres; for knowledge renders military enterprises less doubtful, and obviates many difficulties which seem insurmountable. With such soldiers, the results of well combined operations is no longer left to the chance of events. Moreover, the confidence of the troops in the superiority of their tactics, will render their conduct in the field always more or less satisfactory, and will maintain, with their reputation, the honour of the several regiments, and the glory of the arms of the empire.

★★★★★★

These are excellent views with regard to the advantages of drilling, and skill in manoeuvring. The prodigies performed at Ulm and Austerlitz have shown sufficient grounds for appreciating the results of such a system. S.

★★★★★★

MARCHES AND EVOLUTIONS IN COLUMN.

Marches and evolutions executed in column, form the essential parts of military tactics. In such cases, commanders of battalions and of platoons cannot pay too much attention to all that relates to the direction of the march, to the perpendicular of the flank pivot where the guides are, to the distances between the platoons or the divisions of which the columns are composed, and to the intervals between the different battalions or regiments, in order to give the commander-in-chief the facility of deploying in every direction; resuming the line of battle either to the front, or on one of the divisions or subdivisions of the centre, or on one of the two flanks; and of executing, in fine, all such movements, facing to the rear of the original direction, or by a counter-march. (The distances and covering of the guides, are in fact the ground-work of the march in column.—S).

EXAMPLES OF THE MARCH IN COLUMN TO OUT-FLANK ONE OF THE WINGS OF THE ENEMY'S LINE INTENDED TO BE ATTACKED.

1

The attack with four regiments being directed against the right wing of the enemy, the general in command shall march his lines by the left; the battalions shall be formed into columns by platoons, the left in front, at whole or half distance. (An excellent method of outflanking an enemy on either wing.—S.) The columns thus prepared shall, in marching forward, take a diagonal to the left, and by heads of column formed by each battalion. So soon as the three first platoons shall have taken the given direction, the remainder shall insensibly resume the perpendicular by moving obliquely to the right. The heads of columns marching on the diagonal to the left, having now sufficiently approached the point fixed on for outflanking the enemy's line, and by a rapid movement resumed the perpendicular, shall re-form the line of battle by a general wheel to the right.

It will be advisable, if circumstances admit of it, to keep the columns at the distance of only a half battalion or division from each other, in order to shorten the movement; and also, to close the platoons to half distance whenever the columns change their direction. By such means, a too great undulation will be avoided.

2

If, however, the diagonal to the left, taken by each column, should not prove sufficient to outflank the enemy's right wing, the commander-in-chief must form his new line by successive battalions, beginning with the right of his two lines and giving the following word of command:—"By the right of the two lines, and by successive battalions form line of battle to the right."

The first battalion having executed its movements by platoons to the right in line of battle, shall advance twenty-five paces, in column by platoon, in order to establish itself upon the oblique line indicated for this movement. The other battalions shall successively continue to march until the right of each is parallel with the left of the last formed battalion. They shall then execute a conversion by platoons to the right, and successively take up their proper position in line.

If the attack be directed against the left wing of the enemy, the lines shall march by the right, the columns having the right in front. This measure is applicable to manoeuvres I. and II. It is necessary, during the march of the columns on the diagonal, to designate the last battalions of the two lines as the regulating battalions, when the left is in front, and the first battalions, when the right is in front.

Care must also be taken to make the columns of the second line march so that their heads be directed between the interval of those of the first line, without, however, losing the distance in line prescribed to them. But the moment the columns march directly forward, those of the second line shall resume the perpendicular.

23

Plate 1.

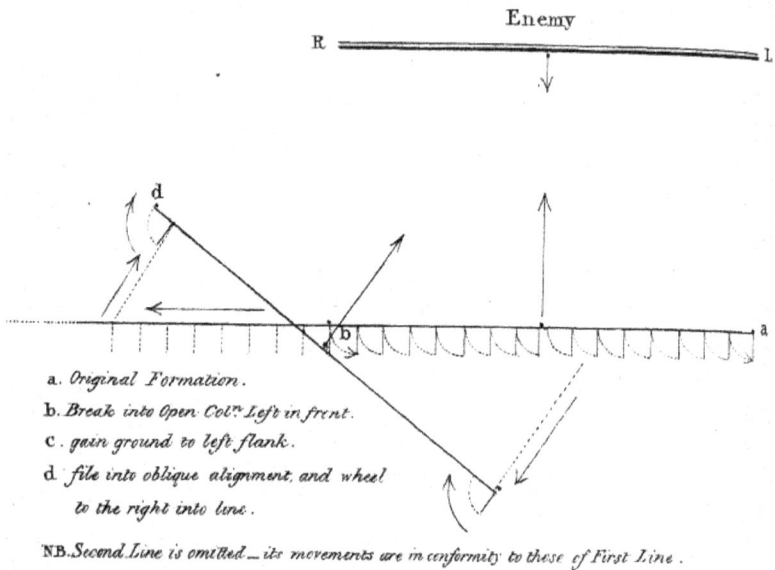

Enemy

R _____ L

a. *Original Formation.*

b. *Break into Open Col.ⁿ Left in front.*

c. *gain ground to left flank.*

d. *file into oblique alignment, and wheel to the right into line.*

N.B. *Second Line is omitted — its movements are in conformity to those of First Line.*

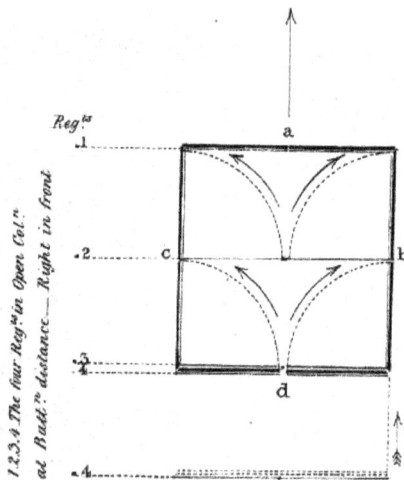

1.2.3.4. The four Reg.ᵗˢ in Open Col.ⁿ at Batt.ⁿ distance — Right in front

Reg.ᵗˢ

a. *Front Face.* b. *Right Face.* c. *Left Face.* d. *Rear Face, viz 4.ᵗʰ Reg.ᵗ faced about.*

4. 4. *The Fourth Reg.ᵗ closed up to form Rear Face.*

3

The enemy being drawn up parallel to the front of your four regiments, and it being the intention of the commander-in-chief to deceive them with regard to the true point of attack,—if it is meant to be on the enemy's right, the battalions of both lines shall form by platoons to the left, and march on, appearing thus to retreat. So soon as the heads of the two lines shall have extended the space of one or two battalions beyond the enemy's front, a new oblique line shall be formed in the following manner:

On the command, "Form the oblique line, left wing in front,"—the fourth platoon of the third battalion of the first line, and the eighth platoon of the third battalion of the second line, or such other platoons as may be directed, shall march by the right flank, and by file to the right; as shall likewise all the platoons preceding those which serve as the axis of the movement, upon the new line taken. The platoons in the rear shall move by the left flank, and form perpendicular to the head. A general wheel to the right will replace the line in the order of battle prescribed.

4

If, on the contrary, the commander-in-chief determine to attack the left of the enemy, the battalions of the two lines shall march to the right, and, as soon as the heads of the columns of the two lines shall have extended the space of a battalion or two beyond the enemy's front, he shall form an oblique line, right wing in front, upon the eighth platoon of the second battalion of the first line, and upon the eighth platoon of the first battalion of the second line. All the divisions preceding those designated for the formation of the oblique line shall operate successively by the left flank, and form on the new line; those in the rear shall operate by the right flank, in order to resume the distance and perpendicular of the head. A general conversion to the left will replace the line in the order of battle prescribed.

5

But if the two heads of columns of the lines, the right being in front, should come to the diagonal on the left towards the centre of the enemy's front, and you intend to attack the left of the enemy's line;—in that case the platoons preceding those which are to serve as the axis, shall operate by the right flank, and those in the rear by the left flank; and, the perpendicular being taken, the line shall be resumed by a general wheel to the left.

Nevertheless, if, during the movement, the enemy should make a demonstration of attack, it would be prudent to form the platoons in the prescribed line of battle, as they successively came up, for the purpose either of making head against the enemy, or of protecting the manoeuvre. (The same project of out-flanking the enemy by simple and sure means—in column, and by one to the left, or one to the right in line of battle.—S.)

If, on the contrary, your heads of columns arrive, the left in front, upon the diagonal on the right, and proceed towards the enemy's centre, and you intend to attack the right wing of the enemy's line,—all the platoons preceding those which serve as the axis in the two lines, shall operate by the left flank, those in the rear by the right flank; and the oblique line of battle shall be re-formed by means of a general conversion of platoons to the right.

6

The four regiments marching in column of platoons, the right in front, on a line parallel to the enemy's front, as if they intended to attack the enemy's left-wing, when, on the contrary, their right wing was the object of attack: in such a case, the oblique line might be formed, the left wing advanced on the first platoon of the third battalion of the first line, and the eighth platoon of the third battalion of the second line, or such other platoons as might be selected; the platoons preceding these, to operate by the right flank, and to proceed along the new per-pendicular; the platoons in the rear, to operate by the left flank and by file to the right.

A general wheel by platoons to the left would place the line in the order of battle required.

It is to be observed that this movement must either be rap-idly executed, or take place at some distance from the enemy, because, for a time, the column stands with its rear to the latter.

The same manoeuvre may also be performed if the lines march in columns of platoons towards the right of the enemy's line, though the commander-in-chief intends to form his oblique line upon the enemy's left. In this case, the platoons in the rear of those fixed upon as the axis of the movement, shall operate by the right flank and by files to the left; those in front of the axis shall operate by the left flank. The perpendicular being assumed, the line of battle shall be re-formed by a general conversion to the right by the two lines. Whenever the commander wishes to change the perpendicular of the columns, he will take care to establish, as in a change of front, the platoon designated for the rest of the troops to form upon.

SOME MANOEUVRES BY MEANS OF THE COLUMN.

1

Four regiments in columns with intervals, marching, right in front, by platoons or divisions, at whole or half distance:—If the commander requires to make them march by front of regiments in columns, on the reverse flank of the guides in natural order, he shall give the following command after halting:—"By platoons (or divisions) on the uneven or alternate battalions of each regiment, to the right form line of battle."

This movement being executed, he may resume his line of battle by a change of front on the centre of each regiment, the right wing forward: that is to say, on the first division of the even battalions of each regiment. But if he wanted to form into line of battle by an inversion of regiments to the other flank, the change of front must be effected with the left wing forward; that is to say, on the fourth division of the uneven battalions of each regiment. If he wished to march in column of regiments by the proper pivot flank, he must execute a conversion of the divisions or platoons by inversion to the left.

2

By this disposition of columns of regiments, the commander might easily form his four regiments into a hollow square. If such were his intention, the first regiment would stand fast; the uneven battalions of the second and third, must execute a conversion to the right by battalions, or by platoons half-wheel to the right, and the even battalions must effect a conversion to the left. The fourth regiment, after having closed its ranks, would form the rear face. The square may march in any required direction, and be reduced on the same principle on which it was formed.

3

The commander having reduced the square in order to form into line in the same order of columns, the first regiment shall operate by platoons to the right after having cleared the second regiment; the latter shall then advance the space of one division, in order to form the basis for the general line. The first regiment shall halt and form in battle; the third and fourth shall operate to the left by platoons, and place themselves successively in the alignment.

If this is to be effected in front on the second regiment, the column shall close to division distance, after which, forward and wheel.

But if the commander intended to form two lines, the uneven regiments would stand fast, whilst the even numbers executed the movement above indicated for the third and fourth regiments.

4

Should the commander, however, find that the movements prescribed for the manoeuvre No. 4 are too slow of execution, he may form a single column of regiments. He will command to form close column, the right in front, upon the colour division of each battalion; and, having closed in mass, he may form into line by battalions in mass, or deploy on any named battalion. (This is the manoeuvre adopted by the regulation of the 4th of March 1831, the movements in mass being preferred in this regulation.—S.)

5

The four regiments having deployed, and the commander being desirous instantly to form two lines, and to place the uneven battalions in the first, and the even battalions in the second, he shall form close columns of regiments, the right in front, on the fourth division of the uneven battalions, then close the masses, at the distance of a battalion from each other, upon the second regiment, and afterwards form into line upon the colour division of each battalion.

But if the general in command wished that the even battalions should form the first, and the uneven battalions the second line, the close columns would form on the first division of the even battalions, left in front; the masses would be closed to battalion distance, and the deployment would, in like manner, be made on the colour division of each battalion.

6

If the commander wants to march in columns, with the left in front, by entire regiments in their proper order: (let us suppose that the odd battalions are in the first, and the even battalions in the second line;) he will command a change of front to be effected on the colour platoon of each battalion, right wing in front. If, on the contrary, he wished to march with the right in front, the change of front must be effected upon the colour platoon of each battalion, the left wing in front. The battalions would thus be in line of battle by inversion.

If the even battalions were in the first, and the uneven battalions in the second line, the column might be formed by fronts of regiments in columns of march, the right in front, by effecting a central change of front in each battalion, left wing forward; and, on the contrary, a change of front, right wing forward, if the troops were to march with the left in front. In this case the battalions would likewise be in line of battle in inverted order. (At present the column is always first formed, even for a change of front.—S.)

7

The line of four regiments or eight battalions being fully deployed, as in manoeuvre No. 5, if the intention of the commander be to make the eight battalions march in two contiguous columns in order to conceal his force and give greater compactness to his movement,—the regiments shall form, in the rear, into columns by divisions, *viz.*: the first regiment with the left, and the second with the right in front. The same movement shall be adopted for the third and fourth regiments. This movement may be executed by the following command:—

On the left of the uneven regiments, left in front, to the rear in column; and on the right of the even regiments, right in front, to the rear in column.

MARCH IN LINE AND INCREASE OF FRONT.

1

The principles of the march in line are clearly enough indicated in the regulation of 1791. The men and the battalions are placed square to the front, on the ground they occupy, and in perfect alignment; the colours are generally carried six paces in front, when the line is to march, for the purpose of giving the cadence of the step, serving as a point of intermediate direction, and preventing the battalions from bulging out beyond the one appointed to direct the movement.

This arrangement, though good in itself, is seldom observed in actual warfare.

★★★★★★

The marshal endeavours to avoid the evils admitted to exist in the old system of marching in line of battle, and he gives the means of doing so. But at present the formation into column by battalions is preferred, even for marching in line of battle.—S.

★★★★★★

The regiments shall continue, nevertheless, to follow this mode, and also the following, which appears to me better adapted to render the direction visible to the whole of the line, and to facilitate the correctness of the line when the word is given to halt.

On the cautionary command:—"Battalions (or lines) will advance," the colours remain in the ranks; the regulating battalion shall advance three paces, so that its rear rank be exactly on a line with the battalions to the right and left. The general guides, or camp colourmen, of the other battalions, shall advance to the same alignment. At the word halt! the whole shall line themselves on the directing battalion. Whenever the first line is to charge bayonets, the directing battalion shall not move from its place in line of battle.

As, on many occasions in war, great advantage may be derived from increasing the front of the line, the commander may effect it in the following manner:—

Let us still suppose four regiments or eight battalions upon one or two lines, and that the front is to be increased by some battalions on the wings.

If it is to be of the four battalions placed at the two wings on the first line, the third rank of those battalions shall go to the right about, retire thirty paces to the rear, front, then quickly forming into two ranks, proceed in double-quick time to align on the first platoon of the first battalion. There shall be a lieutenant and two non-commissioned officers to the third rank of each platoon. The non-commissioned officers shall be placed to the right of the sections, and the lieutenant shall act as captain.

An adjutant-major shall command the two battalions of each regiment thus formed, and to which four drummers shall be attached. The formation shall be the same for the third rank of the two battalions on the left, but the platoons shall execute the inverse movement. These battalions may be employed according to circumstances. (Excellent method of passing from a formation of three ranks to a formation of two, in order to extend the line.—S.)

Passage of Lines.

The passages of lines may be effected by column in different ways, besides those specified in the regulations:—

1

Two lines of four or eight battalions having to execute the passage of lines to the front by column: the first line stands fast; the battalions of the second, having broken into platoons to the right, shall march forward, change the direction to the left by heads of columns of battalions, pass outside the right of the battalion on the first line, and replace themselves in order of battle, either upon the first platoon or division, or upon one of the divisions or subdivisions of the centre. But if the commander wishes positively to place the first line on a parallel with the second, the heads of columns, after they have passed the right of the battalions of the first line, shall oblique to the left in a sufficient degree to regain the platoon front which they have lost by the direct march. This manoeuvre is applicable either to the first or to the second line.

★★★★★★

The method of passage of lines, in the regulations of 1791, was quite defective; the marshal substitutes a mode of doing it in proper columns, which is much more rational. The manoeuvre in the regulations of the 4th of March 1831, is very like that of the marshal.—S.

★★★★★★

The battalions of the second line may likewise gain ground to the front by proceeding round the left of the battalions on the first line. In this latter case they will break by platoons to the left, and will change their direction to the right on reaching the level of the left of the standing battalions.

The movement to the rear is executed in the same manner: the battalions of the first line, after facing right about, and by platoons to the right, march forward, change their direction to the left and pass round the left of the battalions of the second line, and so on by both lines alternately.

2

The passage of lines to the front may likewise be effected by columns of whole regiments for both lines. In this case the second line must form a close column of regiments, the right in front, either upon the first division of the even battalions, or upon the fourth division of the uneven ones. Each column shall march forward and pass through the interval between the two battalions of each regiment of the first line which precedes them.

After having gained sufficient ground, each column shall form into line upon one of the divisions prescribed for its formation. The passage of line of regiments of the second line may likewise be effected by the latter executing the movement of the passing the defile forward by the centre. This mode is perhaps preferable, because the manoeuvre takes up less time, and the heads of columns may immediately execute the platoon firing.

The passage of line retrograde, by columns of regiments, would be evidently too dangerous very near the enemy. Those prescribed by "the regulations, and those indicated in No. 1. for columns of battalions, must, therefore, alone be put in practice.

In the supposition of a general attack in front, the heads of columns of each regiment of the second line, shall march up to the intervals between the battalions of the regiments which precede them on the first line, and thus uniting the *ordre profond* to the *ordre mince,* necessarily give more vigour to the ensemble of the charge. The movement being concluded, the regiments shall extend to the front.

CHANGES OF FRONT.

The changes of front upon one or more extensive lines are seldom executed in actual war. Nevertheless, as most of these movements are effected by the column, I shall give some examples of the manoeuvre.

1

Four or eight battalions, on one or two lines, having to execute a change of front perpendicularly or obliquely, the right wing forward, either upon the centre, or nearer one of the two flanks of the line:—

If the lines are composed of four battalions, the first line shall form the close column of divisions, the right in front, upon the first division of the third battalion, and the second line upon the first division of the second battalion.

If there are eight battalions, the first line shall, in like manner, be formed by column upon the first division of the fifth battalion, and the second line upon the first division of the fourth battalion.

The columns being formed upon either supposition, all the divisions in front of that of formation of the first line (first division of the third battalion, or first division of the fifth battalion,) shall resume the distance from the head or right of the column;

and all those in the rear of the division of formation, after the facing about, shall resume the distance from the rear or left of the column; and then, in succession as the divisions resume their distances, they shall front.

Immediately after the movement of the first line is begun, the second shall march forward, taking its distance from the head, and shall establish itself parallel to the first line. (The method here proposed is much superior to that in the regulations of 1791, and very much resembles that adopted in the new regulations of 1831.—S.)

A general conversion by divisions to the left will place the two lines in the exact order of the change of front commanded.

This movement might be effected by platoons, and its execution rendered much more rapid.

The principle of a change of front, as it may be perceived, remains the same as that laid down in the regulations: that is to say, that if the first line operates it upon the fourth battalion, the right wing forward, the second line executes it upon the third battalion; in like manner, if the first line executes it upon the third battalion, the left wing forward, the second line effects it on the fourth battalion, and so on.

2

Four or eight battalions upon two lines intending to execute a change of front with firing, breaking successively to the rear by platoons or divisions from one of the two wings, in order to form a new oblique line upon one of the flanks:—

When the order for this movement is given, the first division of the battalion on the right of the first line shall operate by the left flank, and by file to the rear by the left; it shall proceed in its whole depth, then face to the right, and march forward, taking a direction behind the front, in order to place itself in line of battle on the extreme left of the line. So soon as the first division has passed to the parallel of the centre of the second division, this latter shall likewise make its movement by the left flank, and so on with regard to the other divisions.

The moment a battalion of the first line has unmasked the front of a battalion of the second line, it shall immediately be replaced, and so on. The battalions of the second line shall execute the fire commanded for those of the first, but none of these battalions shall fall back until the battalions of the first line have executed their movement; after which, if the commander wished to prolong the line, by adding the second to it, he must command the latter to execute the same manoeuvre; or, lastly, by the same movement he may replace it in its position of battle in second line. If the movement is to be effected by the left of the line: in that case the fourth division of the last battalion must move by the right flank and by files to the rear by the right, so as to proceed behind the front, in order to replace itself by the left in battle towards the extreme right of the line, and so on with the other divisions.

3

Changes of individual fronts by battalions give infinite facility in executing the principal manoeuvres of war. They occupy two or three minutes only, and, consequently, they enable the commander to change the front of his line in a very short time, either by executing an oblique change of front upon each battalion, the left wing forward, re-forming afterwards upon the battalion on the right of the first line, by battalions forward in line of battle; or the right wing forward, re-forming upon the last battalion forward in battle. Lastly, this oblique arrangement allows of attacking by order of echelons.

PASSAGE OF DEFILES AND BRIDGES.

The passage of a defile to the rear, by the flank and by files, according to the regulation, is in general very long, and borders too much on confusion to be executed in the presence of the enemy. This movement may be effected in column by sections, platoons, or divisions, either to front or rear. (This reason is the same as the one stated in the new regulations, in which the method presented by Marshal Ney is adopted.—S.)

1

To pass a defile to the front from the centre, according to regulation, the first battalion proceeds by sections to the left, the second, by sections to the right; they afterwards march forward

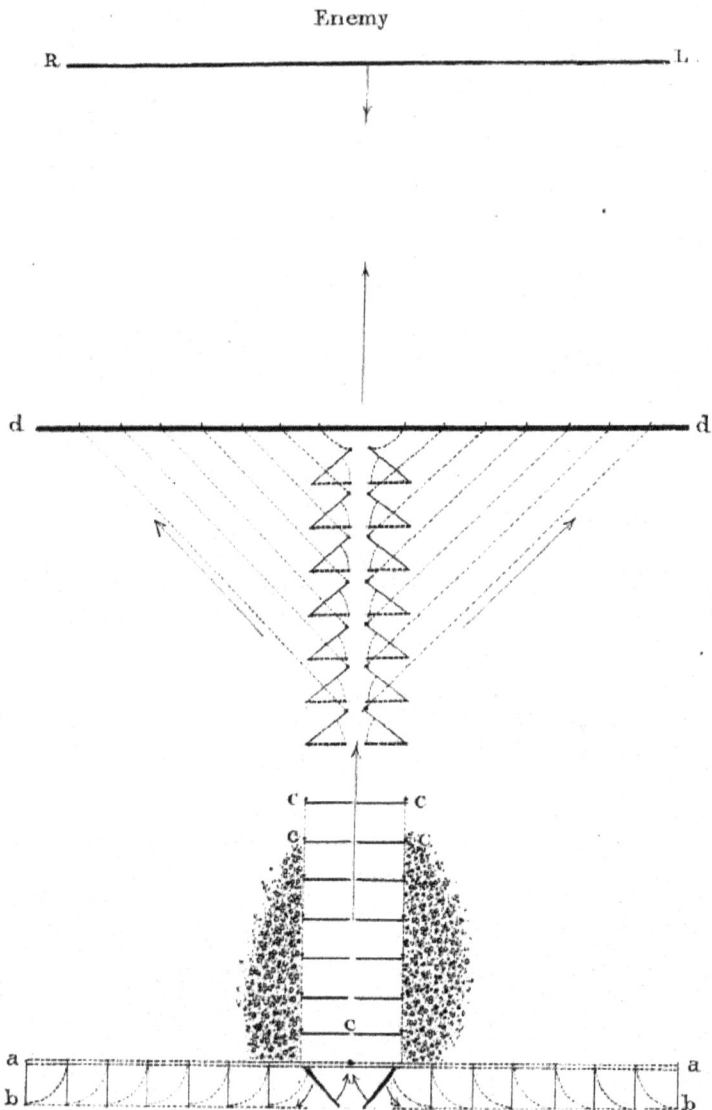

Plate 2

Enemy

R   L

d   d

c   c
c

c

a   a
b   b

a.a. *Original Line. — Facing the Enemy.*

b.b. *Wheel back by Sections, Platoons, or Divisions. — Right wing on the right, Left Wing on the left.*

c.c.c.c.c.*March by platoons &c from the centre thro the defile.*

d.d. *Line reformed on the two centre divisions.*

and form up into line as the defile widens.

Here a battalion is supposed to be posted behind a defile whose width would not allow the passage in front of more than one platoon at a time. In this case all the sections of the half battalion on the right would wheel back into column, the left in front, behind the second section of the fourth platoon; and the sections of the half battalion on the left into column, right in front, behind the first section of the fifth platoon. The battalion marching in this order of column of attack, at section distance, through the defile, should gradually re-form upon the centre and forward in line of battle, as the defile became wider.

2

If the defile is wide enough to allow the free passage of a division in that case all the platoons of the right shall form into column, the left in front, at platoon distance, behind the fourth platoon; and those of the left, with the right in front, behind the fifth platoon. The advance in line of battle shall be executed in the same manner as that specified for the column, by fronts of platoons formed by the sections of the half battalions on right and left.

This mode may be applied to a line of several battalions, by forming the uneven battalions into columns by sections or platoons, the left in front, and the even battalions the right in front. In this case the columns must be closed, so that there remain only an interval of three paces.

3

The passage of the defile in retreat, is effected in the natural order of the sections, platoons, or divisions, in the following manner:—

As the battalion is to break backwards by sections of the two wings at the same time, let us suppose that the defile is behind the second section of the fourth, and first section of the fifth platoon. All the sections of the right wing shall break successively on the left backwards, then front and march; those of the left, on the right backwards, then front and march. On reaching the entrance of the defile, the sections of the right shall make a conversion, or wheel to the left, and the sections of the left a conversion to the right, proceeding together on the new line indicated.

To cover the retrograde movement, it will be necessary for the platoon or division at the entrance of the defile to march up twenty-five paces to the front, and throw out some *tirailleurs*. Lastly, so soon as the two wings have effected their movement, the platoon in advance shall recall its *tirailleurs* by the rallying beat of the drum, and after facing about, place itself three paces in front of the centre of the battalion, and there serve as a base on which to form the general line.

★★★★★★

This method may possibly appear preferable to that indicated in our evolutions. Sec. 87, No. 2, or Sec. 144, No. 2; because the platoons continue fronting the enemy till it comes to their turn successively to wheel back.

★★★★★★

4

If the retrograde movement is to be effected by platoons from both wings of a regiment at the same time, the eighth platoon of the first battalion, and the first platoon of the second battalion, shall likewise advance obliquely to the left and right, in order to cover the point indicated for the passage of the defile to the rear. The platoons of the right, and those of the left of both battalions, shall break to the rear in the same manner as the sections, and the line of battle shall be re-formed in the manner already specified.

If, instead of breaking by platoons, the commander thought proper to break by divisions: in such case the fourth division of the first battalion, and the first division of the second battalion, should execute the same movements.

To aid the judgment of commanders of battalions and platoons as to the distances they are to observe during the march, and to enable them to ascertain when they are to halt, so that the line shall not offer too extensive a development at the moment of conversion to the left to enable the platoons coming from the right, and of wheel to the right for those marching from the left, to resume their order of battle, they shall count as many

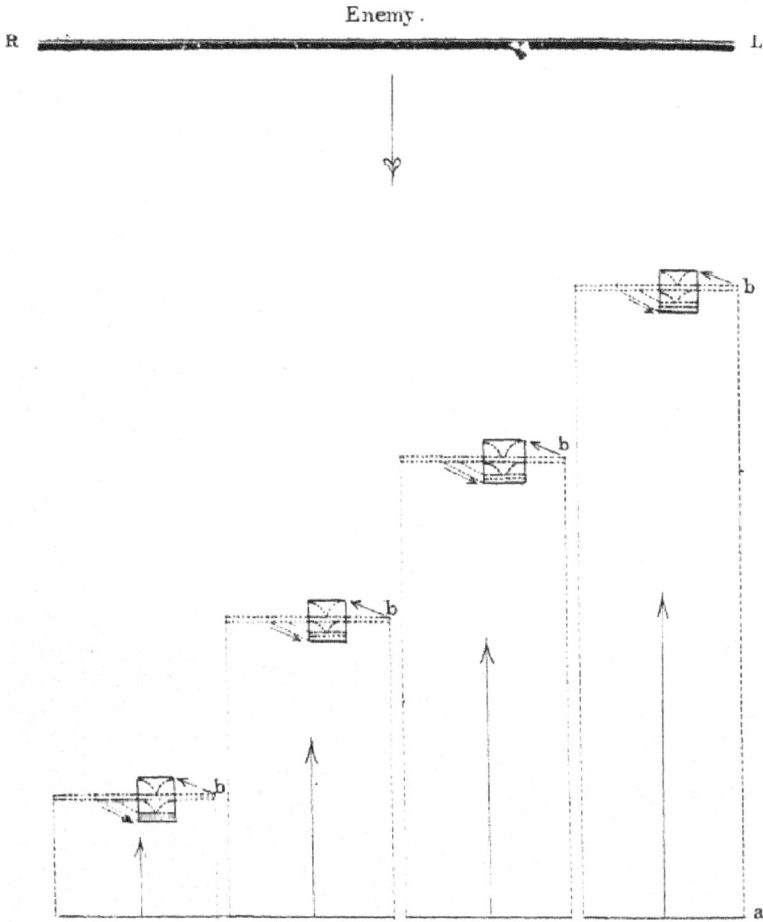

Plate 3.

Enemy.

a. Original Formation — Four Battalions in line.

b. march up in direct Echellon of Battalions to the Front from the right — halt and form Squares, Right in front.

paces as there are files in their platoons, and then multiply by the number which are to follow them, deducting those which are keeping the enemy in check. By such means the commanders of battalions will find no difficulty in halting and forming in line of battle, exactly parallel to the original front of the line, by a general conversion to the left.

MARCH OR ATTACK BY ECHELONS.

This manoeuvre is extremely advantageous in war; but it requires great perfection in the marching of the troops, in order that the attack upon the enemy may be supported with rapidity and intelligence, and that the battalions which refuse the attack may be in a fit state to execute attentively every movement which circumstances may require.

1

Eight battalions upon two lines having to attack the right wing of the enemy placed parallel to their front:—

The movement shall begin by the left at full distances, either by regiments or by battalions, whichever may be preferable. So soon as the last battalion of the first line has marched forward, it shall be followed by that of the second line, and so on by the remaining battalions.

In the supposition that the enemy refuses its right, and makes a demonstration of attack with its left upon the right flank of the echelons in march: in this case, all the battalions shall effect together a change of direction to the right by battalions; or for the sake of more compactness and greater celerity, a change of front upon the colour platoon of each battalion in the two lines, left wing forward.

This manoeuvre being performed, the battalions may continue the attack by echelons, or march forward and place themselves in line of battle upon the first battalions of the right of the two lines, which serve as pivots or *points-d'appui*. By this operation the two wings act alternately on the offensive. (This is a beautiful manoeuvre, and has been adopted in France.—S.)

If the attack were to be made on the left wing of the enemy's line, the movement must begin by the right of the two attacking lines. The change of direction by battalions must be executed to the left; or the change of front made right wing forward.

2

If the commander wishes to attack with only the first line in echelons of battalions, either by the right or by the left, the battalions shall march at full distances, after the echelons are established; and if they were threatened with an attack by cavalry, each battalion should form into column of division at platoon distance, the right in front, upon the colour division of each battalion, if the movement were effected by the right of the line; or the left in front, if the movement were effected by the left of the line. This being done, the first division of each head of column would stand fast. The uneven platoons of the second and third divisions should then wheel to the right, and the even platoons wheel to the left. The fourth division should close up, and then face about so as to form squares by battalions placed in echelons.

3

The attack in echelons by the centre, is in general too dangerous a manoeuvre to be frequently used in war, unless the commander is certain that the enemy have imprudently weakened their centre to strengthen their wings; and that when he has reached the central position he can maintain it, cut off the enemy's wings, and force them to give battle separately. This attack upon the centre requires great resolution and extreme celerity in the march of the assailants.

Let us suppose a first assailant line of eight battalions: in this case the battalions Nos. 4 and 5 shall begin to march at half distance; the other battalions shall in like manner follow at half distance, so that the movement may be better concentrated. It would be prudent not to make the second line march otherwise than in line of battle, in order that it may serve as a support to the two wings of the echelons of the first line, and be able to relieve the first line thus formed, and protect it in case of necessity.

RETREAT EN ECHIQUIER, OR ALTERNATE RETREAT.

The retreat *en echiquier* upon two lines, may be effected according to the principles laid down in the regulations, by falling

Plate 4.

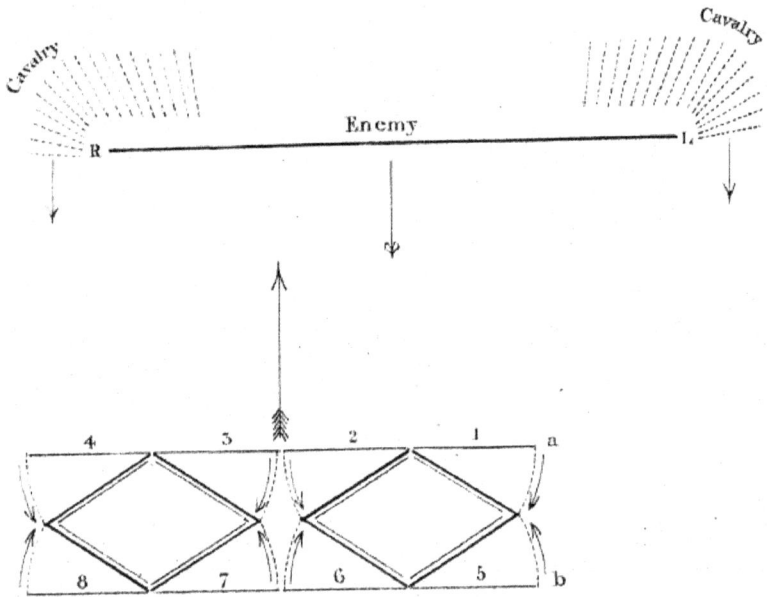

This method of throwing rapidly into Square two lines of Infantry to repel a sudden & unexpected attack of Cavalry... the not included in these Studies, has it is understood been practised by the Marshal. — Batt.ns 1.2.3.4. wheel back 4 paces as represented in the Diagram; & the Battalions of the Second Line wheel up, & face about. This formation is hazardous, & should never be used but in case of dire necessity.

back by battalions a hundred or a hundred and fifty paces. But in order to change alternately the defensive into the offensive, the even battalions of the second line, instead of falling back at the same time as the even battalions of the first line, may form columns by divisions, at either close, half, or whole distance behind the first division, the right in front, and then advance outside the right of the even battalions of the first line then in retreat, and form into line a few *toises* in the rear of the left of the uneven battalions of the first line. This movement may be alternate in the two lines, and by even and uneven battalions, during the whole time that the retrograde movement lasts.

SQUARES.

Squares are formed three deep, in conformity to the emperor's instructions; and sometimes also by doubling up the interior sections, according to the principle laid down in the regulations of 1791. Regiments may also be practised to fire from the four sides by the simple column; and as this is often seen in war, the troops generally marching in that order, it would be advantageous to accustom the men to it.

1

Four regiments crossing a plain in columns with intervals, by platoons or by divisions. If they were attacked by cavalry, and had not time to form into the prescribed squares, the regiments should close up in mass, the three files on the proper pivot flank (it is supposed that the columns have here their right in front) should face to the left flank; and those on the reverse flank should face to the right; the last division would go about. (This formation is adopted in preparing against charges of cavalry.—S.)

2

But if the four regiments marched upon two lines in columns: the first and second regiments of the first line, the right in front, in column upon the eighth platoon of the even battalions, if it be by platoons, or upon the fourth division of the same battalions, if it be by divisions; and the first and second regiments of the second line, with also the right in front, but to the rear in columns upon the first platoons of the uneven battalions, or the

Plate 5.

Cavalry

Cavalry

Enemy.

R

L

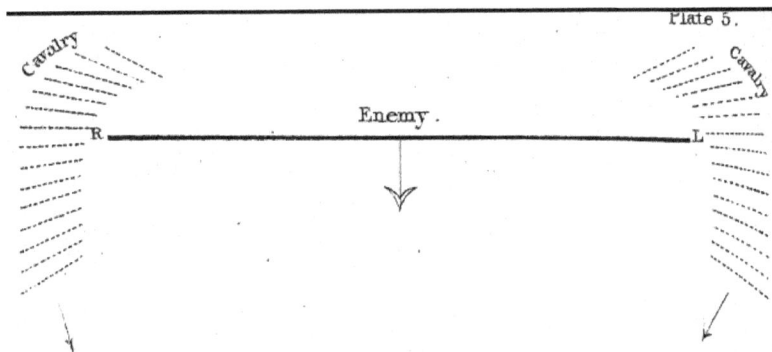

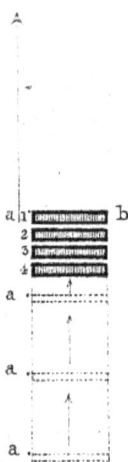

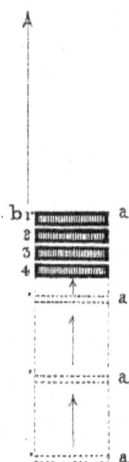

a a a a *Two Col.ⁿˢ of 4 Divisions, at open distance, threatened by Cavalry on the march — close up as at* b . b . — *3 files on pivot flank of ¹/ₜ (and the left) & 3 files on reverse flank, face outwards, — & rear Div.ⁿ 4 go to the right about, and form rear face.*

first divisions of the same battalions, if it be by divisions:—this arrangement would enable the commander to form squares, either by making the uneven platoons wheel to the right, and the even platoons to the left, the column being by divisions at half distance; or, after having closed up in mass, by making the three files on the right and left flanks of the columns face as above to the left and to the right. Should circumstances permit, the *quincunx* may be formed, in order that the fire may cross without inconvenience to the troops.

3

The four regiments may also be formed into columns in the following manner:—The first regiment of the first line forward into column, the right in front, upon the fourth division of the even battalion; the second regiment in the rear into column, the right in front, upon the first division of the uneven battalion. The first regiment of the second line forward into column, the left in front, upon the first division of the uneven battalion, and the second regiment in rear into column, the left in front, upon the fourth division of the even battalion. (The new regulations do not, and very properly so, allow of squares formed of more than three battalions.—S.)

4

Four regiments upon two lines may easily form the hollow square, and place within it the baggage and implements of war, which they might have to cover or protect on a march. In this case, the two lines should leave no interval between the battalions and the regiments.

The first battalion of the first line should break to the rear into column, by platoons, the left in front, at whole distance, upon the eighth platoon; the fourth battalion of the same line into column by platoons, the right in front, behind the first platoon; the first battalion of the second line forward into column, the right in front, upon its eighth platoon, and the fourth battalion forward into column, the left in front, upon its first platoon; a wheel by platoons to the right, by the right flank, would close this part of the square, and a wheel to the left, by the left flank, would close the other part. The second and third battalions of the second line must face about. The grenadiers might be so disposed as to cover the exterior and interior salient angles of the square.

CONCLUSIONS.

Battalions and regiments shall be progressively accustomed to execute all the above manoeuvres, both halting and in marching.

The generals of division shall see that this be done, and shall give to each brigadier-general and colonel under their respective command a copy of these instructions.

As the whole of military tactics lies in the science of forming troops into column with rapidity, and making them march in line of battle, I shall apply myself more particularly to show the utility of making whole lines operate by simple movements in columns of battalions upon one or two lines, and by such means execute all possible changes of front, either from the halt or on the march, comprising generally the principal movements used in war. (Good reflections and excellent principles.—S.)

It is not my intention to develop the knowledge required to carry on warfare on a large scale, but I shall confine myself to the simple mechanism of the evolutions which form the essential ground-work of its particular enterprises. It belongs wholly to the individual genius of the commander to direct his lines of operation in such a manner as to embrace a vast whole; and to be able, at the proper time, to take advantage of all the events and circumstances which succeed each other so rapidly in the field of battle.

The success of every operation in war depends upon confidence of the troops in their leader, which can only be acquired by the example which the general must give when the danger is common to all. He must, without intermission, and with unceasing solicitude, attend to the wants of the men, and insure, by the most persevering activity, the execution of his orders;—nothing being more important in war than to impress upon his army at once, and decidedly, the utmost punctuality in marching at the very moment specified, in order that combined movements may produce the effect intended. False interpretations and misunderstandings put forth by inexperienced men, must be corrected by laconic, clear, and precise orders for movements. It belongs principally to the intelligence of the staff officers to extirpate this military defect, which may lead to so many evils when the remedy is not applied on the instant.

Observations and General Summary.

Columns by battalions at platoon distance, of one or two lines at once, allow the commander to execute every possible manoeuvre, change his direction frequently, and march on the diagonal to the left, the columns having the left in front, and on the diagonal to the right, if the right is in front; likewise to change the direction to the right.

Changes of front by individual battalions are the easiest, because they require only a simple platoon wheel, either in the proper or in an inverted order. Their execution takes up much less time than those indicated in the regulations, and no part of the troops present their rear to the enemy.

Passage of lines by individual battalions forward by the centre.—The battalions of the second line march as in the passage of a defile, forward by the centre, and the forming into line is effected almost without the necessity of any general words of command. The passage of lines, in retreating, does not offer the same advantage; that prescribed by the regulations may be used in preference.

Adjutants-Commandants.

During war, these officers shall be employed in active service and in the army offices, but more especially in the former, in order to select the places of encampment, form the camps, and stake out positions when circumstances admit of it. They are to keep up communications with the headquarters of divisions and with general headquarters; fix upon the places for distributing the provisions, forage, &c.; direct the vanguards, and general and particular reconnoitring parties; proceed with parties to observe the force, the position, and the movements of the enemy. The adjutants-commandants employed in the army offices shall be specially charged with collecting the states as to the situation of

Tirailleur-Chasseur et Flanqueur-Chasseur

GARDE IMPÉRIALE.

the forces; they shall also provide for the wants and subsistence of the men; write reports upon the observations made respecting the country, the topography of the war, marches, encampments, &c. & c., and superintend the *personnel* and *materiel* of the staff.

★★★★★★

The rank of adjutant-commandant does not now exist; but the duties assigned to that officer, and the marshal's instructions, are perfectly applicable to the staff-colonel of the present day.—S.

★★★★★★

The assistant adjutants-commandants shall assist the latter in their important duties. The assistants, to qualify themselves for war, and to benefit as well by their own observations as by those of the other officers in the army, shall write down, in the form of notes, anything that may strike their attention with regard to good or bad dispositions, and neglect nothing to render such remarks profitable to themselves in their profession. The most important thing for a staff-officer is to inure himself to fatigue from the very opening of the campaign, by remaining constantly dressed and booted, in order that, on the very first shot fired, he may be able to proceed in all haste to the place of action, and return and give information to his superiors.

The assistants and other officers of the staff shall be present at every distribution of rations or anything else to the men; they shall reconnoitre during the night in the camps and at the advanced posts. An adjutant-commandant shall regulate the roster of duty, beginning from the head, in everything relative to the service, and from the junior in everything concerning distributions, errands, and other duties of fatigue.

AIDES-DE-CAMP.

Besides the confidence of the general officers, of which *aides-de-camp* must render themselves worthy by indefatigable zeal, it is necessary that they should be extremely active, well acquainted with the different corps of the brigade or division to which they belong, the names of the several officers in command, and

Officier de Chasseurs à pied, grande tenue, Fusilier-Chasseur, tenue de route, et Conscrit, grande tenue.

GARDE IMPÉRIALE.

those of the commissaries, that they may be able to transmit orders with precision, and superintend their execution.

THE COMMANDANT AT HEADQUARTERS.

He shall personally take the orders of the chief of the staff, shall preside at parade, and superintend the interior and exterior duty at headquarters. The watch-word shall be given only in garrisons, such a practice being found useless in camps, where the development is too extensive, especially when several divisions composing a *corps d'armée*, act individually in pursuit of the enemy.

PERSONNEL OF HEADQUARTERS.

The commander of the artillery.

★★★★★★

All that follows, as far as No. 7, is order given to chaos. It was worthy of a mind like that of the marshal to feel the want of this, and to dare undertake it. The principles of this organisation have been adopted in the new regulations for the field.—S.

★★★★★★

A company of guides on horseback, taken from all the corps composing the army.

A company of guides on foot.

Half a company of light artillery.

A company of pontoon men.

A section of miners.

A company of sappers.

A company of armed bakers, and two sections of butchers.

A company of swimmers of a hundred men.

Engineer officers.

Officers topographers.

Commissaries general.

Inspector and sub-inspector of musters.

Officers of health and of pharmacy. The officers of health

Voltigeur et Flanqueur-Grenadier.

GARDE IMPÉRIALE.

shall have *vourches*, (a sort of light car) and shall follow everywhere.

A division of horse *gendarmerie*.

A military commission, or standing court-martial.

Messengers.

Administration of posts, and the veterinary artist of head-quarters.

Paymaster-general, guarded by the guides of the general-in-chief,

Four washerwomen and two sutlers, with carts, each of which shall bear a plate.

INDISPENSABLE OBJECTS ATTACHED TO A GENERAL STAFF.

A bridge equipage consisting of pontoons, another of trestles for crossing a river of from a hundred to two hundred feet wide, provided with cramp-hooks, cordage, anchors, two skiffs, beams, timbers, carpenters' tools, torches, combustibles, pitch, &c. &c.; ladders with cramp-hooks to scale, when necessary, the walls of a town, or other places not strongly fortified by art and nature. The whole placed in drays or other strongly built carriages.

The light artillery attached to headquarters shall always have a good stock of rockets for signals, either to direct night movements, or to guide columns of attack before daybreak, whether in an open country, or when forcing redoubts and entrenchments or storming a fortified place.

An equipage of tumbrils for the provisions and forage.

Baggage of headquarters.—Fix its amount with precision, and preserve the greatest order on a march; and maintain a discipline always difficult, particularly among the soldiers who have the direction and superintendence of the train.

The commander of the equipages, waggons, tumbrils of rockets, bridge-equipages, pontoons, and other implements of war, must be a man of firm character, well informed, and extremely strict. It is necessary that the soldiers of the train should have learned to manoeuvre, in order that, in case of need, the commander of the equipages or of the park, might be able to form

Soldat d'artillerie légère et Vélitc.

GARDE IMPÉRIALE.

a square against the enemy, and to re-form with equal facility into one or more columns. The execution of such manoeuvres requires great rapidity and precision.

THE CHIEF OF THE STAFF.

Besides the staff officers under the command of the chief of the staff, the number of which is fixed by laws and decrees, there shall be an under chief of the staff, who shall superintend the work in the offices, the execution of reports, the destination of troops, and draw up papers upon the reconnoitrings, &c. &c.

The under chief of the staff shall distribute to individuals alone who are attached immediately to the staff—the billets which the commander of headquarters shall issue to him. The orders respecting the police at headquarters, and all measures concerning the details relative thereto, shall be placarded inside the office of headquarters. The commander of the *gendarmerie*, specially charged with this branch of the service, shall keep a register, in which shall be entered the orders and arrangements concerning the distribution of rations, billets, the interior and exterior service, the police, sutlers, washerwomen, prisoners of war, spies, delinquents belonging to the army, convicts, execution of sentences, recruits, deserters, &c.

The following order in billeting, once established, shall be invariably maintained during the war.

The under chief of the staff shall receive from the commandant of headquarters, or from the commander of the *gendarmerie*, billets for the general officers, artillery officers, officers of engineers, assistants, *aides-de-camp*, adjutants, commandants, and other persons immediately attached to the general headquarters.

Billets distributed by the commander of headquarters or under chief of the staff,—To the officers or subdivision of *gendarmerie*, for the non-commissioned officers and *gendarmes*.

Commander of the guides,—To the horse and foot, guides, and the half company of light artillery.

Commander of the *gendarmerie*,—To the sutlers and washerwomen.

Commander of engineers,—To the sappers and pontoon-

Chasseur à pied, grande tenue d'hiver, et Officier des grenadiers à pied en petite tenue.

GARDE IMPÉRIALE.

men.

Commissaries,—To the bakers and butchers.

Commandant of the artillery,— To the swimmers and the reserve park of artillery.

Paymaster,—To the clerks, and other individuals attached to the treasury.

Director-general of posts,—To the messengers and administration of posts.

Inspectors of the administration of bread, liquors, and forage,—To that administration.

The guard of general headquarters, and of the chief of the staff shall be furnished by the horse and foot guides.

The guard of the general in command of the artillery, by the horse or foot gunners.

The guard of the commandant of engineers, and all field officers of that arm, by the sappers, pontoonmen, miners, and swimmers.

The guard of the inspector and sub-inspector of musters, by the bakers and butchers.

The guard of the commissary-general, and the other commissaries, by the bakers and butchers.

The guard of the general administration of posts, by the guides of headquarters.

The guard of the administration of bread, meat, liquids, and forage, shall consist of a detachment of infantry taken from the division nearest to headquarters.

The guard of the treasury to be taken from the guides of general headquarters, or to consist of grenadiers attached to the general staff.

STAFF OF A DIVISION.

The general of division.—The chief of his staff, taken from among the adjutants-commandants; two generals of brigade, two adjutants-commandants, and four assistants.

The commandant of headquarters selected from among

Grenadier à cheval, soldat, grande tenue, et Officier, petite tenue.

GARDE IMPÉRIALE.

the field-officers of the division, or from among the unattached field-officers at home.

A division or sub-division of *gendarmerie* to carry on the police; the commander of this corps is to communicate with the commander of the *gendarmerie* at general headquarters.

Pontoonmen, sappers and miners, to be taken by detachments from those employed in the army.

Two officers of engineers employed in military reconnoitring, constructing military works, tracing and staking out camps and positions, drawing plans of the ground and of marches, engagements, &c. &c.

Paymaster of the division.

Officer in charge of the topographic department.

A bridge equipage of trestles for crossing a river from one to two hundred feet wide, together with a skiff, anchors, cordage, beams, timbers, carpenter's tools, combustibles, torches, scaling ladders to storm a place; rockets to direct the columns during the night, or to serve as signals on a day of battle, engagement, crossing a river, &c. &c.:—

A company of bakers.

One of butchers.

One of swimmers.

Commissaries.

Inspector and sub-inspector of musters.

Commandant of artillery.

Commandant of engineers.

Waggon equipages for the carriage of provisions.

Administrations of posts, bread, liquors, and forage.

Officers of health, surgeons, compounders of drugs.— The surgeons shall follow everywhere either in *voursches* or on horseback.

A company of grenadiers to guard headquarters, and a detachment of a hundred foot soldiers to be alternately on

Chasseurs à cheval (les Guides), petite et grande tenue

GARDE IMPÉRIALE.

duty with the baggage, waggons, administration of posts, &c., and to supply sentries for the post, the inspectors and sub-inspectors of musters, the commissaries, the paymasters, &c.

Composition of a Division in Infantry, Cavalry, and Artillery.

Four regiments of the line, forming two brigades.

One regiment of light infantry, employed in the vanguard.

Four regiments of cavalry, *chasseurs*, dragoons, or *cuirassiers*.

One regiment of *chasseurs* or hussars, employed in the vanguard.

Two companies of light artillery, detached among the infantry brigades; and a half battery for the vanguard.

Eight pieces of heavy artillery, twelve and eight pounders, and six or eight inch howitzers.

A park of reserve, with the necessary ammunition, containing cartridges for infantry and cavalry, besides those required for the light and heavy artillery.

★★★★★★

This organisation must depend upon the country in which the war is carried on, the troops opposed to you, the resources at your disposal, and the object in view. In other respects the proportions are excellent.—S.

★★★★★★

The grenadiers of the whole division may be united so as to form the reserve of the division, to which the heavy cavalry and artillery may be attached.

It is necessary that the park of artillery should be provided with grenades, and the grenadiers exercised in using them, for the storming of a work, a fort, a garrisoned place, &c.

In order to form the staff officers, an adjutant-commandant shall have the command of the vanguard. He shall be relieved once a month by another, and successively by the field-officers of the line.

The other divisions shall be, as much as possible, of the same

Fusilier-Grenadier et Tirailleur-Grenadier (premier régiment)

GARDE IMPÉRIALE.

composition as the above.

The division shall be commanded by the chief of the staff of the army, a general officer, one or more colonels of regiments of the line, *chefs-de-bataillon*, and *chefs-d'escadron*, who shall alternately be officer of the day to superintend the execution of orders with regard to the service of the advanced posts, the camp, the police, the night rounds, &c.

On Encampments.

The regiments of infantry distributed in the different brigades which are to compose the division, or those composing several divisions of the army assembled in a single position, shall be placed in the order of their numbers one, two, three, and four, from right to left, unless particular reasons should prevent this arrangement, which, however, is strictly to be followed if the ground admits of doing so, in order to efface any impression of preference, and prevent jealousy. The French armies are too tenacious of the point of honour to render it prudent in any general officer to grant distinctions to such or such regiments.

The light infantry shall be invariably, placed in front of the line, on the flanks, and sometimes in the rear of the camp.

The cavalry, in the rear and upon the flanks of the line of encampment.

The light cavalry, with the vanguards.

The light artillery, in front and upon the wings of the line of encampment.

The heavy artillery, in the intervals between the brigades, and in reserve behind the line.

The reserve, behind the line, where shall be assembled the park of artillery, the provision waggons, the baggage, &c.

The *baraques* or huts, whether built of boards or of straw, shall be placed in lines of two or three ranks. The distance prescribed between each and between the different battalions and regiments, for the purpose of preventing fire, shall be strictly observed. The same shall hold good with regard to the cavalry and the artillery. The area of the camp shall be marked by stakes driven into the ground, as shall likewise the communications

Garde d'honneur (sous-officier), tenue de campagne, et Éclaireurs.

GARDE IMPÉRIALE.

with the vanguard, the detached posts, body of reserve, place for distributing rations, headquarters, &c. &c.

The fasces of arms shall be formed fifteen feet in front of the flag of the line of huts. The firelocks shall occupy the development of the platoons to which they belong; the cartouches and sabres shall be sheltered as much as possible from the damp and rain by means of sheds made of boards, or covered with thatch.

The colours and drums shall be placed in the centre of the firelocks of their respective battalions.

Each infantry regiment shall have, on the right and left of its front, a pole, at the end of which shall be nailed a board with the number of the regiment inscribed.

The colonel shall have, near his hut, a similar pole showing his name.

The cavalry shall be cantoned, if the locality; allows it, but always near the camp. In the contrary case, the horses shall be picketed in two ranks, and the men have their huts in the rear of them. The front and rear shall be kept clear in order to facilitate the falling in. For this purpose, openings shall be left between the squadrons.

The colonels of cavalry shall, as well for their regiments as for themselves, adopt the method of poles showing the numbers of the regiments and the names of the colonels, as prescribed for the infantry.

The artillery shall follow in every respect the same arrangements that are prescribed for the infantry and cavalry; so also, shall the vanguard and the reserve.

The guards shall be so stationed as to maintain tranquillity, watchfulness, order, and cleanliness in the camp.

The fires for cooking shall be placed according to the sinuosity of the ground, either in the front or in the rear of the line of encampment.

The privies upon the flanks.

SERVICE OF THE CAMP.

The drums shall beat the *reveillé* from two till three in the morning; at four the troop or assembly, when the men shall take

Aide-de-Camp attaché à l'état-major général, et Gendarme d'ordonnance.

GARDE IMPÉRIALE.

their arms, form in front of the colour, and be ready to execute any movement which circumstances may require. In the event of a manoeuvre, the guards of the camp and the police guards shall receive notice to remain at their respective posts. They shall prevent any stranger from entering the camp. But if the troops do not manoeuvre, they shall be dismissed at broad daylight, after having been inspected.

The trumpeters shall sound the *boute-selle*, or "to horse," immediately after the beating of the *reveillé*. The horses shall be saddled and prepared, at four the bridles shall be put on, and the cavalry regiments shall, in the greatest silence, fall in at the place indicated for that purpose. The colonels shall order the captains to have the rolls called, and if at broad daylight there is no manoeuvre to be performed, the squadrons shall return to the camp in the same order, after the inspection of clothing, accoutrements, harness, and arms.

The heavy artillery shall put the horses to the guns at the same time that the cavalry mount, and the gunners shall be ready to march.

The light artillery shall mount, and the horses be harnessed to the pieces.

All these arrangements shall be equally applicable to the rearguard, the waggons, the baggage, and all, in short, belonging to a *corps-d'armée*.

The vanguard shall have its duty diminished during the day, in order to be more active and alert during the night. As soon as the day closes, the videttes shall be doubled. A service of patrols shall be established in such a manner, that there shall always be some on duty. If there are different outlets to guard, leading to the principal post, they shall be barricaded with ladders, felled trees, or waggons without wheels, and be further guarded by squads of infantry. The cavalry shall guard the advanced posts during the day, and occupy the most advanced positions in the neighbourhood.

At nightfall, they shall withdraw to a good distance in the rear of the infantry, and only four or five cavalry orderlies shall remain at the principal post of infantry, to carry to the commandant of the camp intelligence of any attack that may be made upon the vanguard. At daybreak, the cavalry shall scour the country according to the orders it may receive, and the infantry remain under arms till its return. It is very necessary that a detachment of cavalry of the new guard should, in reconnoitring, accompany the one relieved, in order to become acquainted with the localities and with the inequalities of the ground.

The order of the day shall be given out after parade, or in the morning immediately after inspection.

The generals and staff-officers shall proceed to the camp at four in the morning, when the troops fall in. They shall remain until the return of the reconnoitring parties.

The service of the camp and of the advanced posts shall begin at the *reveillé*. The posts shall remain doubled, until the return of the reconnoitring parties sent in the direction of the enemy; and if there is nothing new, the relieved guards shall return to the camp.

If the troops in the camp are to march against the enemy, the colonels of regiments, and even the officers and non-commissioned officers, shall write in their pocket-books the principal dispositions for the attack which they will have to operate. For it is not indifferent to an officer anxious to do his duty properly, to know the right, the centre, and the left of the brigades or divisions of the camp with which he will have to act, and more especially the hospitals for the wounded, the places where the rations are to be distributed, and lastly, the point on which the reserve park of artillery will be stationed during the skirmish, engagement, or battle.

The report of the officers of the day shall be addressed to the chief of the staff of their division, who shall forward it to the general staff.

The firelocks shall be drawn as soon as the advanced guards have returned to the camp. The adjutant-major of each battalion shall assemble, for this purpose, the men just come off guard, and shall receive back the ball-cartridges. Each soldier shall be furnished with a pricker to clear the touch-hole of his piece, two flints garnished with sheet-lead, and placed in reserve in the pocket of the cartouche, a cloth to wipe the pan, and a small phial of oil to keep the lock in order.

The cavalry soldiers, besides being provided with these articles, as necessary to the carbine as to the musket, shall each have a small hatchet in the left holster, instead of a second pistol. This hatchet consists of a hammer and a blade in the shape of a half moon, formed of a single piece of metal. At the bottom of the handle, there shall be a screw-ring to enable the rider to fasten his horse to a tree, &c. This screw shall be fixed inside the handle by means of a *matrice* formed therein.

Colonels of infantry and cavalry may, on days of rest, have the different classes of recruits drilled, and the infantry exercised in the drill of platoons and battalions, the cavalry in that of squadrons. The officers and non-commissioned officers shall be instructed at least twice a week, in the theory relating both to the manner of giving the word of command, and the execution of evolutions and grand manoeuvres, and also in the military rules and the administration of military bodies.

It is then that colonels well versed in the art of war shall examine them on points of knowledge necessary for the attack and defence of a fortified place, the attack and defence of a post, reconnoitring to be effected in an open or wooded country, and lastly, on the different occurrences in war in which the duties of officers are so important.

The cavalry officers and non-commissioned officers shall be instructed in the theory of their own arm. The cavalry shall take care during the war to have two horses in each squadron with pack-saddles, to which shall be fastened two baskets lined with strong leather, containing a stock of cartridges for the carbines, muskets, or other firelocks; also, spare flints, and worms for drawing charges.

The guardrooms shall be established at the advanced posts, and the men guilty of breach of discipline shall be sent thither. These shall have no huts, and shall receive nothing but dry bread, with the exception of soup twice a week.

The code of penalties and military crimes shall be read every Sunday at the head of each company.

The retreat shall be beat at specified hours; the band shall play an hour beforehand in front of the fasces of arms, the colours and the drums, and in the centre of the battalions.

The roll shall be called immediately after the tattoo, and the fires extinguished at tattoo at eight or nine o'clock at night; or at ten o'clock, when soup is to be served out, &c. In the cavalry, the rolls shall be called four times a day; in the morning when the men mount their horses, at noon, at two o'clock, and in the evening before the horses are dressed. The same regulations apply to the infantry, to whom, every regulation relating to the service and to the police, is likewise applicable. The cavalry shall have, if possible, pickets with iron points, to picket the horses in camp or at bivouac. But the laxity of discipline during actual service is the cause that this article, so necessary to cavalry soldiers, is seldom preserved more than a few months, because it is inconvenient to the men when in the ranks.

The soldiers shall be exercised in making fascines, saucissons, gabions, and in constructing works necessary in a campaign, such as entrenchments, redoubts, &c. The officers shall endeavour to acquire skill in directing these works, in order to be able to entrench themselves with detachments, in case of need, for the defence of a post, or a wood, or a village, or a defile, a bridge, a river, a ford, &c. The sentries and videttes shall be accustomed to place themselves at night in holes which they shall dig. This plan, besides sheltering them from surprise, enables them to hear at an immense distance the approach of anyone, by listening from time to time with the head reclining in the excavation.

Both infantry and cavalry shall supply night pickets, who, every evening before the tattoo, shall assemble behind the hut of each colonel, to be employed as circumstances may require.

The cavalry shall send patrols during the night along the great communications in the rear of the camp, and along those of the different headquarters.

DISTRIBUTION OF RATIONS.

The chief of the staff shall issue an order of the day, stating the arrangements relative to the distribution of rations, whether for two, three, or four days. When rations are to be distributed, each regiment shall send an armed detachment with the fatigue-men whose turn of duty it is, and also the adjutants and under-officers. The corps shall be mentioned which in their turn take precedence in the distribution, consisting of bread, meat, rice, salt, dry vegetables, brandy, wine, vinegar, forage, straw, oats, &c. Water shall also be sent for in a regular manner; the fountains, springs, wells, and brooks in the neighbourhood of the camp shall be guarded by posts of infantry.

The cavalry shall proceed to the distributions in the same order as the infantry, and shall have, to water their horses, a place different from that resorted to for water by the infantry, and which shall be guarded by a mounted vidette.

The staff officers shall be directed to be present, by turns, at the issues, for the purpose of preserving good order there, and examining the quality of the bread, meat, forage, liquids, &c. Articles of bad quality, spoilt or unwholesome, shall not be paid for to the contractor, provided there be a *procès-verbal* requiring that they shall be burnt. The receipts of the adjutants and quarter-master sergeants shall be given to the storekeeper in the presence of the quartermaster general and the commissary-general, both of whom are to be present at the distributions.

On the March of a Corps d'Armée, a Division, a Brigade, a Reconnoitring Party, a Patrole, &c.

A body of troops shall never leave the camp except on a formal order of the general in command, and in presence of the staff or other officer appointed to carry the order into execution, after having examined the instructions for the direction of the march and the nature of the enterprise.

If the expedition is not a secret one, it is necessary that the commander of the detachment should read the instructions, and make, in case of need, such reflections and observations upon them as he may think proper, and which the staff-officer shall report to his general, if he be not attached to the expedition, in which case he shall forward them by a cavalry orderly.

When a *corps-d'armée* is preparing for a movement, either for offensive operations, or to effect a retreat, the men shall fall in without the least noise, an hour before the march. The generals of brigade shall march at the head of their respective columns, and the staff-officers, before the troops engage, on the flanks and in the rear, in order that the officers of regiments may remain in their places of battle, and that the distances may be well observed without allowing the depth of each column to lengthen out.

Each regiment of infantry and of cavalry shall form a rear-guard, commanded by officers of firmness, and notoriously devoted to military discipline. This guard is to prevent the number of stragglers from being too great, and force the men to keep to their ranks. The soldiers under arrest, in confinement, or in the guardhouse, shall march at the head of the battalions to which they belong, with their coats turned, their muskets slung reversed on their backs, without bayonet, or sabre, or cartridges.

They may be made to engage with the *tirailleurs*; so soon as the action begins, ammunition and bayonets may be given out to them. After the action they shall return to the guardhouse, unless their colonel forgives their fault on account of their good conduct during the action. The men thus in confinement shall be forced to perform all the drudgery of the camp, field works, &c.

The vanguard shall proceed with all the precautions necessary to ensure a march, and discover by its flankers the situation of the enemy. It shall open its march with a squadron of light cavalry, a company of carabineers, an eight-pounder, or a four-pounder; a battalion of light infantry, three squadrons of light cavalry upon the flanks of this battalion of light infantry, behind which shall be two pieces of artillery: a howitzer and an eight-pounder, remaining artillery, and the march shall be closed up by the cavalry. The piece of cannon at the head of the column shall be fired as rapidly as possible the moment the enemy is perceived in force, in order to give notice to the *corps d'armée*. A staff-officer shall be immediately despatched to the general in command, to report on what has been perceived of the enemy's force, position, or motions.

The *corps d'armée* shall march, so far as the nature of the ground will permit, by platoons or divisions, at half distances, and even in columns of half-battalions or battalions, if the country should become more open, and when the position which the army is to occupy by a rapid attack requires that it should form into line of battle with great celerity. The cavalry stationed in the several divisions shall march on the roads upon the flanks and in sections, or by fours.

The battalions shall maintain a distance of twenty *toises* from each other, the regiments a distance of sixty *toises*, and the brigades a distance of a hundred and twenty *toises*. But, to ensure precision in this arrangement, staff-officers, or adjutants-major from the infantry regiments, and intelligent orderlies on horseback, shall be stationed so as to prevent the columns from becoming encumbered, or from stopping during the march. If the enemy is far off, there shall be a general halt of half an hour after every two hours of march. If it be a forced march, it shall continue four hours, and then a halt of an hour for refreshment.

It is necessary to accustom a number of non-commissioned officers, placed along the whole depth of the column, on the pivot flank, to repeat the word of command "halt," from the head to the rear, if the column is to stop, and the march is by files, sections, platoons, or divisions; also the word "march" after the halt, when the command to resume the march is given, &c. This very simple measure is of the greatest importance.

The drummers and fifers shall, during the march, be distributed at the head of their respective battalions. A number of them, fixed by the drum-major or by the corporal-drummer, shall execute different beats accompanied by the fifes. By day only, and when the enemy is far off, the bands shall remain at the head of their respective regiments, and shall play, from time to time, different warlike airs. The cavalry trumpets shall play flourishes; the march shall be commanded by sound of trumpet, and the sounding of a call shall suffice to stop the column. The march shall be resumed, whenever it can be so managed, only after the men have had their soup.

The greatest order shall exist in the march of the baggage and the provision waggons, which shall be guarded by a detachment of infantry and cavalry, taken either from the reserves of the different divisions, or from the army in general. The guard of headquarters, the commissariat, the *gendarmerie*, the sutlers, &c. shall follow in the order laid down by the commander-in-chief.

The park of artillery, the bridge-equipages, and the other implements of war, shall always remain with the reserve, to which also shall be attached the surgeons and the moveable hospitals.

General Instructions Relative to the March of One or More Divisions of a *Corps-D'Armée*.

Order of march for the . . . . .

The division of the general commanding the vanguard, or the brigade forming the vanguard, or, in fine, the flankers, shall quit the position of . . . . . at two o'clock in the morning precisely, with arms and baggage. It shall march with the right (or the left) in front, secure its march and its flanks, maintain the greatest order in its movements, and proceed to the camp, place, position, &c. of . . . . . fixed upon and staked off by the engineer and staff-officers, in pursuance of instructions to this effect. It shall place its right . . . . (after having established! its advanced posts in a line with . . . . .) on the village behind the . . . . . brook, its centre upon the heights of . . . . and its left shall extend to the forest of . . . . , whose outlets and skirts it shall guard. Its reserve, park of artillery, and baggage, shall be stationed in the rear of the village, at the river or wood of . . . . . and the headquarters of the division shall be established at . . . . .

The first, second, third, or fourth division shall quit its camp and proceed to . . . . . and, on reaching its position, shall connect by posts its right with the left of the first division, and its left with the right of the third division: thus the first division shall occupy the position of . . . . . the second division that of the third that of . . . . . and the fourth, &c. The reserves shall be established in the best manner possible in the centre and rear of their respective divisions. The headquarters of the first division shall be at . . . . . those of the second, third, and fourth, &c.

The reserve of the army shall occupy the position of . . . . . the grand park shall be at . . . . . in the rear of the centre division of the army. (Name the headquarters of the reserve and of the commander-in-chief of the artillery.)

If the army marches in different columns,—which is almost always the case in actual service, in order as well to accelerate the march, and facilitate the providing of food, as to act upon a great extent of front—the order of march shall specify the direction of each, the particulars of its position of encampment, and its flanks—so that a service of patrols and reconnoitring parties may be established, to prevent the enemy from throwing a large force between them and engaging them separately, or from taking them in flank or in the rear.

The columns ordered to flank the army shall detach a battalion, two pieces of light artillery, and two squadrons of light cavalry, under the command of an adjutant-commandant, whom the general of division may send to reconnoitre the ground which the division is to occupy, and who shall report to this general any discoveries he may make during his expedition.

The generals of division shall be careful to transmit to the general-in-chief a report of every circumstance which may occur during the march. This latter shall specify the division in which he will remain on the day of a battle, engagement, or march. All reports shall be written or made verbally by the *aides-de-camp*, each of whom shall be provided with a pocket-book, in which he shall write the reports, and also the orders to be given to the different corps.

The strictest orders shall be given that no musket shall be fired during the march of a column. If the firelocks have been loaded for some days, the adjutant-major shall assemble all the men of the battalion, and have the whole of them discharged together.

Everything captured from the enemy shall be sent to the headquarters of the division, and thence to general headquarters. It shall be stated in general orders that the proper staff-officers shall deliver specific receipts, whether on the arrival of prisoners of distinction, or on the delivery of pieces of cannon, colours, standards, or any other implements of war. The receipt shall specify the sum allowed by the general-in-chief for each article, and these sums shall be paid by the paymasters of the divisions to the quartermaster of each regiment, and under the authority of the *conseil-d'administration*, which shall certify the propriety of each claim. A staff-officer shall be appointed exclusively to superintend the prisoners of war, their removal to the rear of the army, and their exchange if necessary. His proceedings shall be certified by a register, countersigned through each page by the chief of the general staff. This officer shall receive the sums of money sent to our own prisoners of war, and those received for the prisoners we have captured.

A Day of Engagement or of Battle.

All the grenadiers of brigades, of divisions, or of the whole army, shall be assembled to form corps of reserve, and decide the fate of the battle by an act of vigour. This arrangement is equally necessary whether the field of battle be a plain or a country intersected with ditches, woods, and other obstacles.

All the troops shall, if circumstances admit, undergo a strict inspection before the battle; and the generals shall harangue the men and excite each to do his duty. They shall state the rewards which the government confers upon such as distinguish themselves, and invoke the justice of their cause, which must make them triumph over the enemy.

The generals and field-officers of corps shall remain at their respective posts, in order to execute the movements and manoeuvres ordered by the general-in-chief. The generals may, on that day, increase the number of their staff, by taking an officer and a non-commissioned officer from each regiment of cavalry; and an adjutant-major, or an adjutant non-commissioned officer, on horseback, from each regiment of infantry, to transmit orders and reports to the generals who command them.

All important reports shall be conveyed to the general-in-chief by an *aide-de-camp* attached to the adjutants-commandants, or by an officer of correspondence. Each of these shall take care to write in his pocket-book the order to be executed, or the report to be made, in the event of the general transmitting them being unable to write and sign a letter or note.

The baggage, equipages, provision waggons, &c., shall, during the action, be assembled in the rear of the reserve; the armed detachments taken from the camp shall return to their respective corps, the reserves acting as the guard. The park of artillery, the bridge-equipages, and the other implements of war, shall never quit the reserve; but should the latter have to engage, the commander of the reserve shall leave a battalion or a squadron to serve as a guard of safety, and shall take care to give notice to the commander-in-chief, by despatching a mounted officer.

The hospitals shall be distributed along the right, the centre, and the left, so as to receive the wounded whom the officers of health attached to the several divisions may send thither, after having put on the first dressings. Should the number of wounded increase, so that any one hospital were overfilled, the commander of the reserve should give a sufficient guard to the director-general of the hospitals, to enable the latter to assemble in all haste a number of waggons belonging to the country, sufficient to contain the sick. The removal of the wounded from the hospitals must be made slowly, and with the greatest care.

The men killed in the field of battle shall be immediately buried, or removed from the sight of the soldiers. But if the battle were long, and the loss of life very great, it would be expedient, after the victory, to have a funeral ceremony for the burial of the brave men who had fallen, and even to erect monuments in commemoration of the battle. Nothing tends more to increase the strength and confidence of an army than the conviction that when a soldier is wounded, great care will be taken of him, and if he falls, his memory will be honoured by a funeral ceremony; that he will, in short, be consigned to the grave, with all the honours granted to those slain in the field of battle.

Never, under any circumstances, shall a soldier quit his ranks, unless he be seriously wounded. The repairs necessary to his arms often serves as a pretence for leaving the field of battle. The officers and the non-commissioned officers in the rear shall pay the strictest attention to this. They may replace arms that have become unfit for service by others taken from the killed or wounded.

Each regiment shall have one or more waggons to collect

the arms that want repair and those taken from the enemy. The armourers shall render the former fit for service at the first regimental halt, and the others shall be sent to the office of the general staff. It would be better to break them to pieces than to leave them at the disposal of the inhabitants of a conquered country, who would often return them to the enemy, or even use them against the army, if there were any negligence in picking them up and carrying them away in waggons.

The most rigorous orders shall be given that no wounded soldier shall be carried by his comrades further than the first hospital. Two men shall suffice for a fracture, and one for a slight wound.

They who have itch or syphilis shall undergo medical treatment in the hospitals which follow the general headquarters.

Colonels of regiments shall take care to deliver with great pomp the arms of honour awarded by the government to the non-commissioned officers and privates who have distinguished themselves in battle. They shall parade the regiment under arms, and make a speech suitable to the occasion. This plan leads to prodigies of valour.

Punishments for cowardice likewise require an imposing form. If an officer, non-commissioned officer, or private, is guilty of it, he must be publicly degraded in the presence of the whole regiment paraded without arms. The colonel's speech must be short, but energetic, in order to excite the love of glory, and deprecate with horror that cowardice which shames and disgraces the army and the nation. It is requisite that every regiment should have three provosts to perform such military executions.

Regiments losing their colours or standards, their cannon, or their colonel, shall have no others during the campaign, unless they make an equivalent reprisal from the enemy.

Pieces of cannon, colours, standards, baggage, and other implements of war taken from the enemy, shall be paid for, exclusively of the reward given by the government, at the rate fixed by general orders. This sum shall be paid by the *conseil d'administration* of each regiment, to be distributed among all the non-commissioned officers and privates who compose the same.

During battle, the regimental band shall assemble in the rear of the regiment, and play warlike airs. The trumpeters shall sound flourishes: the drummers and fifers shall be sent to the right and in the rear of their respective battalions, in order to execute the beats which the colonel may direct. The sappers shall be assembled on the right of the regiment, to be employed wherever their services may be requisite. They shall be armed with firelocks, besides their hatchets. Their officers shall carry a brace of pistols, in a belt round the waist; they shall also have a small cartouche, with the number of the regiment upon it. Each officer, non-commissioned officer, and private, shall wear the number of his regiment upon the facings of his coat.

After the battle, each colonel shall minutely inspect his regiment, as well to ascertain what men are present, as to ascertain the state of their arms and accoutrements. Those men who remain absent four days from the regiment without good cause, shall be placed in confinement, and shall forfeit their pay during the period of such confinement; the sums thus forfeited shall be applied to the minor articles of equipment for the men of the regiment generally.

The colonels shall address to the chief of the staff of their respective divisions, and the latter to the chief of the general staff, an exact statement of the losses sustained by their regiment, its prisoners of war, its killed and wounded, its captures from the enemy, &c. They shall do their best to make such reports as circumstantial as possible, and shall include the whole of the occurrences of the battle, manoeuvres, changes of position, charges, retreats,—every movement, in short, executed during the action.

When the enemy is retreating, and the line has received the command to halt, the regimental bands must execute airs of victory, and the cavalry trumpets sound flourishes. Nothing gives greater relaxation to the men than this, and nothing urges them more strongly to deeds of heroism. If at this moment the colonels can issue a small ration of wine or brandy to the men, it would add to the general excitement. Wine is always to be preferred, because it gives real strength without injury; whereas brandy is only good for night marches, or just before the attack of an important post, a redoubt, an entrenchment, a storming, &c. &c. But when success is obtained, it is prudent to relieve the men who have won it by others who have taken no share in the action. A man adapted to such desperate service and such *coups-de-main*, is scarcely ever able to display the same energy in defence as in attack.

If the victory gained is of sufficient importance to fix the attention of the commander-in-chief, the troops shall be either assembled immediately after the battle, or on the following day. Guns shall be fired in token of rejoicing: the men shall fire five rounds, as shall likewise the artillery, in pursuance of orders to be given for the firing to take place from right to left at the same time. The generals shall be at their respective posts; they shall talk to the men about the national gratitude which the latter have just earned by their valour, and exhort them to continue in the same course, in order to force the enemy to sue for peace. This is always the great object pursued throughout a war.

The intelligence and information possessed by the French armies require that they should be duly apprised of the cause for which they are fighting; and it is only when the aggression is justified by the provocation, that they can be expected to display surpassing heroism. An unjust war is repugnant to the national character; the men, who soon become well-informed on the subject, evince much less courage; and if they suffer themselves to be killed rather than disobey their officers, it is not less true that they no longer show the same energy in dangerous attacks. French soldiers must never be called upon to fight except in a just cause, one founded upon incontrovertible political reasoning, and free from improper motives.

Fragments upon Arms.

The sabre of the foot soldier must be so formed as to be adapted to the barrel of the musket.

In action, many bayonets are broken or carried away by cannon shot; the men, in falling, often bend or break them, and are thus without the means of defence. If a soldier has a sabre-bayonet he is safe. There are situations in war when a man can act neither with his firelock nor with his bayonet, as during the night for instance. He might then carry his musket as the dragoons do their carbines, and use his sabre-bayonet in a confined space where his musket would only embarrass.

The sabre-bayonet shall have a foot of sharpened blade, and a foot and half without being sharpened, in order that the men may not be wounded in loading their pieces. It shall weigh only double the weight of the common bayonet, shall have a light but solid hilt, with a guard which, by means of a spring, shall fold down when the sabre is fixed on the firelock. The socket shall be three inches long, the hilt four inches and half, and the guard, with a spring as aforesaid, in order to admit of the musket being fired. The length of the sabre shall be two feet six inches. (About two feet nine inches, English measure.)

Thus, when the men in the first rank charge bayonets, by applying the lock of their firelocks to their right haunch, which diminishes the length fourteen inches, as they present their arm diagonally,—a musket with the sabre-bayonet would still extend beyond the front of the first line five feet ten inches. A sabre-bayonet in the second rank would extend beyond the first four feet four inches; one in the third rank two feet ten inches.

Let it be observed that eighteen inches are allowed from the first to the second rank, and the same from the second to the third. (The reader must bear in mind that all these calculations are made by French measure, which is larger than the English.) It is not to be presumed that with such a range of bayonet, the enemy's cavalry could break a line so formed; and a charge of bayonets against infantry not so well armed must prove fatal to the latter.

But the men in the third rank, to avoid the danger in making a charge, would not bring down their bayonets to the charge until they were close to the enemy: they would advance porting arms; for if a man fell, as he could not see the ground covered by the first and second ranks, he might wound some of the men in these ranks. Besides, the sabre-bayonet should only be fixed upon the piece at the very moment the cavalry is seen preparing to charge, or at the very instant a charge against infantry is ordered.

The *chasseurs* and hussars, now that they have firelocks, must be in some degree assimilated to the infantry. The carbine shall have a ramrod with a slide or ring at its extremity; and a ring which turns over the muzzle of the piece, so that the ramrod may enter the barrel naturally, without its being necessary to turn it in order to ram down the cartridge. The loading effected, the ramrod brings back the ring to its former position.

In this manner the ramrod is never lost, even when the carbine is hung up by a peg. This kind of ramrod might be adapted to the infantry muskets. To facilitate the taking out of the ramrod, there might be a screw at the extremity, which could be unscrewed at pleasure. The objection is, that if a ramrod were to break, the man could not borrow one from a fellow-soldier. But it is the least of two evils, for most of the detached ramrods are lost.

There must be a single pistol in the right holster, without a ramrod, of the same calibre as the carbine, and a little larger than our common pistols; in the left holster a hatchet so made that the bayonet may be fixed upon it, in order that if the man in close battle should break his sword, he may defend himself with his hatchet, and stab with his bayonet.

These hatchets serve, moreover, for everything the men may want to cut during a campaign: pickets for encamping, or anything else. There must be a screw and a ring at the end of the handle, for the purpose of hanging up the hatchet, or fastening the horse.

The Third Rank of Infantry Considered as a Reserve; Advantageous Use to be Made of It Under Different Circumstances in War.

A line of infantry cannot, without some danger, march to offensive warfare with bayonets charged three deep. Any unevenness in the ground, indeed the least undulation, forms an obstacle dangerous to the precision necessary in such an attack. The bayonets of the third rank might easily wound the men in the first, because they only reach the shoulders of these men; and because the men in the third rank have no facility to distinguish, like those in the first and second rank, the ground which the line has to pass over.

To avoid the danger of this kind of attack, the charge with the bayonet should be made only by the first and second ranks; the third should follow with ported arms. The line having reached the ground occupied by the enemy, should fire without moving from the position of charge bayonets; the third rank, and without any other notice than the firing, should advance as *tirailleurs*. But if the enemy stood the charge, they should not quit their place, but bring down their bayonets to the charge, in order to support and increase the impetus given by the two first ranks.

Supposing a regiment marching in column by sections, platoons, or divisions, to gain a position indicated, and on its way thither to be attacked or harassed by the enemy's cavalry the colonel, to clear and cover the march, may detach the third rank of the three first, of the four last, or of the whole of the divisions forming the column. The third rank of the uneven platoons shall march to the right of each respective division, in either one or two ranks; the rear of the third rank of the even platoons shall, in like manner, flank the left of the column. The same disposition shall be pursued whether the left or the right of the column be in front.

A lieutenant and a drummer from each company shall always march with the men of the third rank when acting as *éclaireurs*.

In the event of a battalion of infantry being attacked by a body of horse (we suppose here that circumstances prevent the battalion from forming into square, which is the only effective mode of resisting such an attack), after the two first ranks have fired, the third shall advance as *tirailleurs*; and when the line has reloaded, it shall follow the impetus given by the third rank, with charged bayonets and in double quick time.

But if the *tirailleurs* were, in their turn, threatened by the enemy, the lieutenants should order the rally to be beat, and form groups, in the centre of which they would maintain themselves, with their drummers, until the arrival of the line. Should the danger continue, the third rank should resume its original station; in the contrary case, it should proceed with its attack.

Some of the enemy's horsemen might perhaps succeed in passing the wings and attacking the rear: in that case the whole should halt, the rear rank face about, and, after firing and reloading, charge bayonets. The two first ranks should then, after firing, reload, and also come to the charge.

If in defiance of this firing the enemy continued their attack upon the front and the rear of the line, the colonel should command the second rank to carry arms in order to fire at will front and rear, or by the even files to the front and the uneven to the rear. The first and third ranks should, in the meantime, remain with the bayonet at the charge until the danger was over. In this situation the supernumerary rank should be distributed in the intervals of the second rank, behind the captains and sergeants closing the third rank. Those over and above might be placed to the left of the grenadiers, and between the seventh and eighth platoons of the battalion.

If a column of infantry were obliged to cross a plain in effecting its retreat, and were attacked by a numerous cavalry, it must form without hesitation into close column by divisions, and then into square, if necessary. The men of the third rank of the sections which have doubled, and of those preceding them, may be successfully employed in advancing from the square to repulse the assailants, and even to cover the march when the danger is over.

When a regiment is drawn up in line, in any camp fixed upon or staked out, the third rank shall advance from the line to any distance determined upon by the colonel in command, in order to cover the line, allow it to form the fasces of arms, and order the service of the advanced posts, pickets, and camp guards. When this is done, the third rank shall resume its place.

If the camp were attacked, the third rank should fall in without any word of command, upon the ground it is to occupy, in front of the line, in order to give the remainder of the regiment time to form and prepare for action. A column of infantry sent to search a wood, or a village, or any other part of a covered country, may, during its march, employ the men of the third rank, without deranging in any way the ensemble of the corps.

Direct and oblique firing are those which, in war, present the least confusion, and allow colonels of infantry best to observe the results, so as to follow up the evolutions which circumstances may render necessary.

In this kind of firing, the front rank kneels. This movement generally displeases the men, and exposes them to ruptures as they rise to reload their pieces. Another disadvantage not less important is, that it prevents the line from charging rapidly with the bayonet. There are but few instances to be cited during the last war, in which direct firing, according to this system, has been executed with any great success. This circumstance alone would militate against its practice.

What matters the period at which the soldiers were first accustomed to execute a dangerous movement? If its execution is disadvantageous in war, there ought to be no hesitation in rejecting the practice.

It has been remarked that when, in dangerous situations, the soldiers have been obliged to kneel, there has been some difficulty in making them rise during the enemy's fire, because they were in some measure sheltered from it; for the most even ground has always some slight inequalities which shelter a man in such position.

The firing of two ranks, or file firing, is, with the exception of a very few movements, absolutely the only kind of firing which offers much greater advantages to the infantry than those above-mentioned. The third rank, during this firing, exchange their loaded pieces with the discharged pieces of the second rank; but this exchange is made with repugnance, and the men of the second rank fire with much less confidence the pieces which have not been loaded by themselves.

Most infantry officers must have remarked the almost insurmountable difficulty they find in stopping file-firing during battle, after it has once begun, especially when the enemy is well within shot; and this firing, in spite of the command given by the field-officers, resembles general discharges. It would be better, therefore, after the two first ranks have fired, to charge boldly with the bayonet, and by an act of vigour force the enemy to retreat.

The German soldier, formed by the severest discipline, is cooler than any other. Under such circumstances he would, in the end, obtain the advantage in this kind of firing, if it lasted long.

This imperfection disappears when the firing is confined to the two first ranks, the third porting arms and remaining as a reserve to be used according to circumstances. It has, moreover, been proved that the best drilled infantry in firing is not, on that account, the best in battle. Ammunition always fails in the end, and this diminishes the men's confidence; each then finds some excuse, either in the condition of his firelock, or even in his own impatience and vivacity, for hastening his retreat, unless the movement becomes offensive.

These observations are of a nature to urge colonels of infantry regiments to prepare and drill their men to attacks by main strength, so peculiarly adapted to the vivacity and temperament which distinguish the French soldier from that of other nations.

After the two first ranks have fired, the third, having reserved its fire, will increase the disorder in the enemy's ranks if they be broken. This rank may be employed with the same success in protecting the retreat of the line, should unforeseen events render a retrograde movement necessary. This reserve, so essential, offers an infinity of resources of which the commander may avail himself according to circumstances.

The firing of infantry, of whatever nature it may be, offers real advantages only when troops are acting on the defensive.

A country covered with wood, intersected with hedges, ditches, defiles difficult of access, rivers, marshes, fords, and bridges, is favourable to this; kind of warfare; for such natural obstacles may be strengthened by redoubts, entrenchments, felled trees, and other field works.

The defensive system is ill calculated for the French soldier, unless his excitement be kept up by diversions and successive excursions. In a word, if the lesser kind of warfare be not constantly carried on, idleness destroys the strength of a body of troops acting merely on the defensive. It is constantly in danger of being surprised day and night; whereas expeditions prudently combined, raise the courage of the men, and prevent them from discovering the real cause of their dangerous situation.

In offensive warfare, the French soldier has inexhaustible resources; his active genius, and his bravery in storming, double his energy; and a French commander ought never to hesitate in marching against the enemy with the bayonet, if the ground is at all adapted to a charge in line with one or more battalions at a time.

It is by attacking that the French soldier is inured to all kinds of warfare, whether when he braves the fire of the enemy, which is seldom very destructive, or when the field is left open to his intelligence and boldness.

One of the greatest difficulties in war is to have the men inured to marching. The other nations of Europe will with difficulty reach the same perfection in this respect as the French, whose abstemiousness and physical temperament are powerful causes which, in this kind of fatigue, have given them such immense superiority over the Austrians.

The rapidity of a march, or rather skilful marches, almost always determine the success of a war. Thus, colonels of infantry ought to neglect nothing to obtain progressive perfection in ordinary and forced marches. To accomplish this object so essential in war, it is necessary to oblige the men to carry their knapsacks from the very opening of the campaign, and also to accustom them to the works attendant upon military operations. The health of the soldiers depends upon this; it will also effect a considerable saving of men who are lost in partial actions, and also prove a great saving in hospital expenses.

It is this power of marching which constitutes the strength of infantry; and enterprises which seem to present the greatest difficulties, become comparatively easy by the advantages accruing from rapid marches.

Most of the infantry manoeuvres executed in time of, peace are not used in war; those easiest to be understood ought to form the basis of manoeuvring, and their execution should be rigorously enforced. The superfluous must be rejected without hesitation, and the leisure of winter quarters, now spent in teaching useless evolutions, which the troops will scarcely ever have occasion to perform even in the course of numerous campaigns, be devoted to instructing the infantry officers and non-commissioned officers. They should be taught the system of attacking and defending fortified places; they should be exercised in the erection of military field works, in attacking and defending a post, in military reconnoitring, &c.; and lastly the *coup d'oeil* must be exercised in the choice of positions and encampments, whether for offensive or defensive operations.

It is admitted by all military men that infantry is the great lever of war, and that the artillery and cavalry are only indispensable accessories. Care ought therefore to be taken that the officers and non-commissioned officers of infantry should be as well informed as possible. The national genius discloses a vast field of resources for this object, and particularly at the present period when promotion is open to all.

The greatest powers of Europe have always shown the most particular and unremitting attention to the drilling and forming of their infantry, without considering the too great number of evolutions invented in time of peace, for the soldiers' torment, by officers often more systematic than experienced in war. Two essential conditions constitute the strength of infantry:—

That the men be good walkers and inured to fatigue.

That the firing be well executed.

The physical constitution, and the national composition of the French armies, fulfil the former most advantageously; the vivacity and intelligence of the soldiers ensure the success of the latter.

The following evolutions, to which the infantry ought to be restricted, both in time of peace and of war, would, I imagine, meet the views of government and the real end of the institution of infantry.

EVOLUTIONS IN LINE.

First part.

Formation of a regiment in line of battle. (The places of the officers and non-commissioned officers in the ranks, and in close order.)

Open and close the ranks.

The manual exercise.

The command and execution of the different firings.

Break and form by files, sections, platoons, and divisions.

Form a line into close column.

Deploy into line.

Second part.

March in order of battle, in close column, and in column of route.

Oblique and diagonal march.

Change of front and of direction.

Passage of defile by wings or centre, either in front, or in rear of the line.

Order in echelons.

Retreat in *échiquier*, or by alternate divisions.

Passage of lines.

Formations against cavalry. (Squares.)

The soldier's instruction in platoon and battalion, ought to be founded upon these evolutions.

In order to facilitate their execution, it would be important, besides exercising the men in the marching step, the ordinary step, and the quick step, to exercise them also in running. This method would produce amazing celerity in the formation of the different columns, and also in the deployments. French soldiers are more calculated than those of any other nation to attain this perfection, which so well agrees with their intelligence.

I think, in summing up my reflections, that it would not be

useless to advise colonels of infantry regiments to avoid, with the greatest care, a reverse at the opening of the campaign. The least check has more influence than is generally supposed upon the remaining operations of the campaign: it diminishes the confidence of the men. by raising mistrust of the commander's talents. The least success, on the contrary, impresses upon the troops, from the very beginning, that just military pride which doubles their strength, and serves as a presage of a series of brilliant feats.

Victory smiles in general upon those only who know how to command it by good preparations. It is seldom the effect of chance or of unexpected good luck, but the fruit and recompense culled by the experienced soldier whose discernment is supported by the resolution and boldness of his undertakings.

Irresolution in war is the most dangerous defect in a commander, more especially when the enemy is approaching. He must make up his mind without long deliberation, and above all things prevent French soldiers from giving way to their propensity to criticism. The most distinguished men in the career of arms have never ceased repeating this axiom:

> Make your preparations for attack or defence *instantly* on the enemy's approach; should you even be obliged to execute them with disadvantage, do not hesitate.

The enemy, who is a good observer, would take advantage of your indecision. It is often better to come to a bad decision immediately, than to hesitate between several good ones; for the bad one has always some favourable side by which success may be obtained. Moreover, a vigilant mind is never embarrassed by the presence of the enemy, which on the contrary will tend to facilitate the boldness of its conceptions.

ON THE ATTACK AND DEFENCE OF ENTRENCHMENTS.

There are three kinds of entrenchments used in war:

Redoubts, or closed works.

Continuous lines.

Detached works, open at their gorges.

Experience has convinced well-informed soldiers, that redoubts, particularly those in the form of a *quincunx*, are to be preferred to all kinds of entrenchments; they are indeed the only ones which suit the French, because they allow of offensive retaliations on the part of those who defend them, which is peculiarly adapted to the national character of Frenchmen.

This species of entrenchment has been used with the greatest success, and has decided the fate of several celebrated battles; those of Pultawa and Fontenoy, for instance, Frederick the Great held them in great estimation; and they were very useful, during the last war, in the entrenched camp of the creek of Ham at Dusseldorf.

Entrenchments, or continuous lines, of which great use was made in the old wars, are adapted to absolutely defensive operations. They are open to the great inconvenience of spreading the means of defence along a considerable extent, and, consequently, of being weak upon all points which the enemy may attack.

They offer moreover the great disadvantage of forcing an army to abandon them the instant any part of them is carried.

The British often use them, and were thus entrenched at the last battle which decided the fate of Egypt.

Detached works ought to be considered simple batteries only, for the employment of the artillery and of some troops. I think they ought not to be used except in the rear of redoubts, and for the establishment of fixed batteries and a part of the reserve. This species of entrenchment is seldom capable of being long defended.

On the Attack and Defence of an Entrenched Camp Formed by Two Lines of Redoubts, in the Form of a Quincunx.

1st, the Defence.

To defend an entrenched camp, the troops must be divided into four bodies: one to be placed in the redoubts, two at a hundred and fifty *toises* behind them, and the fourth to form a reserve.

The redoubts shall be mounted with the necessary cannon. The light and heavy artillery shall be placed in the most advantageous positions.

These arrangements being made, and the enemy having given the signal of attack, the redoubts, which are so many little fortresses reciprocally protecting, though independent of, each other, will necessarily oblige the assailants to break their lines, as well to surround them as to prevent the double fire of their artillery and musketry. If some of the redoubts are carried, and the others sorely beset, then the light and heavy artillery must batter those in possession of the enemy, directing the whole of their fire against them.

Now is the time for the second line to act: it must fall with impetuosity upon the broken enemy, weakened by the exertions they have already made, discouraged by their losses, and surprised that in attacking they become the attacked. This offensive return generally produces a great effect, and forces the enemy to make a retrograde movement. Should the attack of the second line not produce the effect anticipated, the reserve covers its retreat.

2nd, the Attack.

For the attack of an entrenched camp with two divisions of eight battalions each: the troops shall arrive in columns, and form into line out of the reach of the enemy's shot.

The first line, which is that of attack, shall detach about a company from each battalion as *tirailleurs*; to these volunteers, shall be added the sappers of the battalions and of the division, with hatchets, a few hoes, fascines, and light ladders.

The point of attack shall be either on the right or the left, and must embrace two salient redoubts, together with those defending them in the second line.

As soon as the troops are within half cannon range of the enemy, the *tirailleurs* shall advance at a run, and leap into the ditches of the works attacked, in order to cut the palisades and make openings through which they may penetrate into the interior. Meanwhile, the line of attack shall advance in good order with the light artillery, which shall fire as it proceeds, and be protected by the heavy artillery which shall remain with the second division.

The *tirailleurs* must carry the redoubts attacked; if they are not strong enough, they shall be reinforced by a few companies of grenadiers. In no case must the line of attack be broken, in order that it may always be ready to face the enemy's second line and reserve.

The redoubts being taken, the line shall advance rapidly, porting arms; it shall not fire until it is within twenty-five paces pf the enemy, who shall then be instantly charged with fixed bayonets.

The cavalry must follow the division of attack, in order to be in a situation to take advantage of the victory when once the redoubts are taken and the enemy routed.

The second division shall deploy at the distance of cannon-shot, feign an attack upon the left of the enemy's camp, and then advance, or protect the retreat, according as events may turn out.

On the Attack of Entrenchments, or Continuous Lines,
by One or More Divisions.

A division of four regiments, or eight battalions, charged to make the principal attack, shall form into line beyond the range of the cannon of the enemy's entrenchments which they are to storm. Every order for the details of the undertaking must be clear, precise, and laconic. The instant before the attack, the staff-officers having the direction of the columns, shall ascertain whether all the officers clearly comprehend the instructions given, in order to avoid misconceptions, which are always dangerous and sometimes fatal to the success of combined operations. The general officer in command shall harangue the men in a manner suited to the occasion, and with that energy which characterizes a warrior.

All being ready, the signal of attack shall be made by three guns being fired, and the troops shall march to the enemy at the charge, and in the following order:—

The companies of *tirailleurs* of the eighth battalion, the command of which shall be intrusted to a field or a staff officer, shall cover the front of attack. The men shall each be provided with a hatchet besides his firelock; and when within shot they shall run

93

as fast as possible into the ditches of the entrenchments, cut the palisades, tear away the fascines and gabions, and make openings.

An officer of engineers and the sappers of the army attached to this division, shall march with the *tirailleurs* for the same purpose. So soon as the officer shall have reconnoitred the situation of the enemy's entrenchments, he shall dispatch a non-commissioned officer, or proceed himself in all haste to make his report, in order that if circumstance, require it, the plan of attack may be changed.

The sappers of the four regiments of infantry shall be divided into four equal bodies:

The first shall open the march of the two companies of grenadiers formed in column of platoons in front of the first battalion of the first regiment, at a hundred and fifty *toises* in the rear of the *tirailleurs*, and a hundred and fifty *toises* in advance of the column.

The second shall be at the head of the two companies of grenadiers, also in column of platoons, first battalion, second regiment, right brigade.

The third shall be at the head of the two companies of grenadiers, first battalion, third regiment, left brigade.

The uneven battalions shall be formed in column of platoons, the right in front. They shall follow the movement of the grenadiers, observing the prescribed distance of a hundred and fifty *toises*, until the moment the grenadiers arrive within fifty *toises* of the entrenchment. Then, the double quick step to close up and give impetus to the storming.

The men of the battalions in column, and also the grenadiers, shall each carry, if necessary, a fascine under his left arm, to fill up the ditches and be enabled to pass with greater ease the impediments which the enemy may oppose to the attack.

The even battalions shall march in line, carrying arms, at three hundred *toises* from the four columns of attack. The interval occasioned by this distance shall be filled by a squadron of light cavalry.

The light artillery shall be placed upon the two exterior flanks of the columns of attack of the first and fourth regiments, on a level with the companies of grenadiers, whose movements it shall follow within one hundred and fifty *toises* of the enemy's entrenchments.

The remainder of the cavalry and of the artillery of the line shall form a reserve, and march in the second line three hundred *toises* in the rear of the even battalions, in order to be employed as circumstances may require.

An officer of engineers, or of the staff, shall be attached to each column of attack.

After the entrenchments are carried, the *tirailleurs* shall pursue the routed enemy, and clear the interior flanks of their works.

The sappers of the division and those of the regiments shall fill up the ditches, and make openings for the passage of cavalry, at the places pointed out by the officers of engineers or staff officers attached to the columns of attack. The grenadiers shall remain within the entrenchments.

The moment the columns of attack have passed the entrenchments, they shall form as a first line, one hundred and fifty *toises* in advance of the grenadiers.

The even battalions shall pass by platoons, right in front, through the intervals of the first line, then form into line, and charge bayonets on the enemy's reserve, should it still resist. They shall be preceded by *tirailleurs*.

The eight companies of grenadiers shall form the reserve, and march one hundred and fifty *toises* in their rear.

The light artillery and the cavalry shall march on the flanks of the even battalions, now become the first line, constantly developing the enemy's wings; and the light cavalry shall charge as *tirailleurs* whenever a favourable opportunity offers.

If, upon one of the flanks of the principal attack, the ground presents advantages sufficient, several pieces of artillery of the line shall be united to silence the enemy's fire and protect the attack made by the columns.

Should the enemy's entrenchments present a greater development than the front of attack of one division, the second division shall dispose its forces in the same manner, and the third shall march in line of battle in the rear of the centre of the two first, in order to support and protect the attempt.

In the event of failure, the retreat shall be effected in the same order as the attack, until the troops reach the level of the first position; and if by a vastly superior force the enemy compelled a retrograde movement, the retreat should, in such case, be effected *en échiquier.* In this predicament, the cavalry and light artillery should be employed on the flanks, and stationed according as circumstances might require.

On the Attack of Detached Works Covered at Their Gorges.

An army protected by a line of redans or detached works covered at their gorges, is to be attacked at daybreak.

The division of attack shall be formed into close columns of divisions, preceded by some companies of *éclaireurs.*

The columns of attack shall penetrate within the intervals of the redans, and break the enemy, who, being in line of battle, will be unable to resist the shock of the numerous columns by which they are surrounded. The second division shall follow the movement of the first, in line of battle.

LEONAUR

ALSO FROM LEONAUR
AVAILABLE IN SOFTCOVER OR HARDCOVER WITH DUST JACKET

JOURNALS OF ROBERT ROGERS OF THE RANGERS *by Robert Rogers*—The exploits of Rogers & the Rangers in his own words during 1755-1761 in the French & Indian War.

GALLOPING GUNS *by James Young*—The Experiences of an Officer of the Bengal Horse Artillery During the Second Maratha War 1804-1805.

GORDON *by Demetrius Charles Boulger*—The Career of Gordon of Khartoum.

THE BATTLE OF NEW ORLEANS *by Zachary F. Smith*—The final major engagement of the War of 1812.

THE TWO WARS OF MRS DUBERLY *by Frances Isabella Duberly*—An Intrepid Victorian Lady's Experience of the Crimea and Indian Mutiny.

WITH THE GUARDS' BRIGADE DURING THE BOER WAR *by Edward P. Lowry*—On Campaign from Bloemfontein to Koomati Poort and Back.

THE REBELLIOUS DUCHESS *by Paul F. S. Dermoncourt*—The Adventures of the Duchess of Berri and Her Attempt to Overthrow French Monarchy.

MEN OF THE MUTINY *by John Tulloch Nash & Henry Metcalfe*—Two Accounts of the Great Indian Mutiny of 1857: Fighting with the Bengal Yeomanry Cavalry & Private Metcalfe at Lucknow.

CAMPAIGN IN THE CRIMEA *by George Shuldham Peard*—The Recollections of an Officer of the 20th Regiment of Foot.

WITHIN SEBASTOPOL *by K. Hodasevich*—A Narrative of the Campaign in the Crimea, and of the Events of the Siege.

WITH THE CAVALRY TO AFGHANISTAN *by William Taylor*—The Experiences of a Trooper of H. M. 4th Light Dragoons During the First Afghan War.

THE CAWNPORE MAN *by Mowbray Thompson*—A First Hand Account of the Siege and Massacre During the Indian Mutiny By One of Four Survivors.

BRIGADE COMMANDER: AFGHANISTAN *by Henry Brooke*—The Journal of the Commander of the 2nd Infantry Brigade, Kandahar Field Force During the Second Afghan War.

BANCROFT OF THE BENGAL HORSE ARTILLERY *by N. W. Bancroft*—An Account of the First Sikh War 1845-1846.

www.ingramcontent.com/pod-product-compliance
Lightning Source LLC
Chambersburg PA
CBHW032021090426
42741CB00006B/684